Music Is My Business: The Ultimate Startup Guide to the Music Industry

Wally Lockard III

Published by Wally Lockard III, 2024.

MUSIC IS MY BUSINESS: THE ULTIMATE STARTUP GUIDE TO THE MUSIC INDUSTRY

First edition. July 8, 2024.

ISBN: 979-8224825677

Written by Wally Lockard III.

Table of Contents

ABOUT THE AUTHOR ...1

CRAFTING YOUR VISION ...7

ESTABLISHING A BRAND ...8

COMMITTING TO YOUR DREAMS ...9

MAKING YOUR PLAN ...11

KEEPING YOUR PLAN SECRET ...14

FUNDING YOUR BUSINESS ...15

SACRIFICES FOR SUCCESS ...20

BUILDING YOUR SUPREME TEAM ...22

THE FOUR P'S: PAPERWORK, PEOPLE, PROCESS & PRODUCT ...24

WHEN TO UN-FOLLOW IN REAL LIFE ...37

SAYING NO ...38

GOOD ENERGY ...41

STAYING POSITIVE ...43

STRATEGIC PARTNERSHIPS ...45

MAKE YOUR PLAN B TO MAKE YOUR PLAN A WORK ...47

MUSIC BUSINESS POST-COVID ...49

BUSINESS FORMATION ...50

MARKETING IN THE MUSIC BUSINESS ...95

ENTREPRENUERSHIP ...107

MY STORY ...110

BUILD A DREAM TEAM 115

WORK ON YOUR PASSION AND FIND YOUR PURPOSE 117

UNDERSTAND YOUR INDUSTRY AND CATER TO YOUR CONSUMERS... 120

PROTECT AND MONETIZE.. 124

MONETIZE... 131

MUSIC DISTRIBUTION... 137

FAREWELL 145

Dedication

This book is dedicated to all the dreamers, hustlers, and grinders in the music industry. To those whose passion for music ignites their spirit, fuels their ambition, and drives them to break barriers every single day.

To my son, Wally Lockard IV: You are my greatest inspiration and the light of my life. Your boundless energy, creativity, and unwavering curiosity remind me daily of the beauty and power of dreams. May you always chase your aspirations with the same fervor and determination, knowing that the world is yours to conquer.

To my family and friends, your unwavering support and love have been my rock. Your belief in me has been the cornerstone of this journey, and for that, I am eternally grateful.

To my mentors and colleagues, thank you for your wisdom, guidance, and encouragement. Your insights have been invaluable, helping me navigate the intricate maze of the music business with confidence and clarity.

To Urban Grind TV, my award-winning platform that I birthed: You have opened doors to amazing opportunities and provided a tremendous stage for countless talents. Your impact on the music industry and my personal journey has been immeasurable. Thank you for being a beacon of creativity and innovation.

And finally, to every aspiring artist, producer, manager, and entrepreneur out there: May this book serve as your guide and inspiration in the exhilarating world of the music business. Keep grinding, stay true to your vision, and remember that music is more than a business—it's a way of life.

With heartfelt gratitude,

Wally Lockard III, J.D.

ABOUT THE AUTHOR

Wally Lockard III, J.D., a renowned figure from Chicago, boasts over two decades of influence in the entertainment industry. With expertise spanning music, management, television, and media, he's made a lasting impact on urban culture.

A standout achievement is his stewardship of Urban Grind TV (UGTV), a revered Hip-Hop show running for 15 years and 28 seasons on Comcast Cable 25 in Chicago. As its Executive Producer, he's lauded for his visionary leadership, earning the show 26 awards.

Apart from UGTV, Wally has guided music artists to chart success, with placements on the iTunes Top 10 and Billboard Charts, reaching as high as #19. His dedication to showcasing emerging talent and expanding creative boundaries is evident across ventures like Urban Grind Radio, UGTV Music Distro, UGTV Latino, and UGTV Models.

Under Urban Grind Management, Wally leverages his expertise to guide talent and drive innovation. His commitment to education and mentorship is evident through involvement in organizations like the Chicago Music Awards and the Recording Academy. He also contributes to the Triton College Alumni Association.

As Vice President of Operations for Kingz Kounty Media Group in Brooklyn, NY, Wally continues to shape the industry. His military service and induction into the Hip-Hop Heritage Foundation Hall of Fame further highlight his impact.

For updates from Wally Lockard III and Urban Grind Management, visit UrbanGrindTV.com or follow @UrbanGrindTV on social media.

SCAN CODE FOR MORE INFO:

Introduction

Welcome to *MUSIC IS MY BUSINESS: THE ULTIMATE STARTUP GUIDE TO THE MUSIC INDUSTRY*. This book is dedicated to the dreamers, the artists, the entrepreneurs, the producers, and all those who breathe music.

Who is this book for?

This book is your compass, designed for aspiring artists, producers, songwriters, record label owners, studio proprietors, managers, and the hustlers who wear multiple hats in the music realm. Whether you're stepping into the rhythm of creation for the first time or have been orchestrating melodies for a decade, this guide is your roadmap to understanding the minds and maneuvers of serious contenders. In the music business, attitude and perspective are not just assets; they're the currency of success. While technical prowess can be developed over time, strategic thinking from the get-go is non-negotiable.

Why is it essential to finish this book?

Simply put: "You Can't Make Money & Excuses at the Same Time."

Whether you're dipping your toes into the vast ocean of the music industry or diving headfirst into its depths, commitment to the journey is paramount. Your attitude is your greatest asset in navigating the challenges and triumphs ahead. Expect to encounter storms of deception, currents of exploitation, and waves of rejection. But amidst the tempest, remember why you embarked on this musical odyssey. Your resilience, focus, and unwavering passion will steer you through the tumultuous waters. Guard your energy and stay anchored to your purpose.

Key Areas Covered in This Book:

I. Crafting Your Vision

- Clarifying your goals and aspirations in the music industry.

II. Establishing a Brand

- Developing a unique identity and image to stand out in the market.

III. Committing to Your Dreams

- Maintaining dedication and perseverance in pursuing your musical ambitions.

IV. Making Your Plan

- Creating a strategic roadmap for your music career.

V. Keeping Your Plan Secret

- Understanding the importance of discretion and confidentiality in business planning.

VI. Funding Your Business

- Exploring various avenues for financing music projects and ventures.

VII. Sacrifice to Succeed

- Embracing the challenges and sacrifices inherent in the pursuit of success.

VIII. Building Your Supreme Team

- Surrounding yourself with a supportive and talented network of professionals.

IX. The Four P's

- Exploring the principles of Paperwork, People, Process and Product in the music business.

X. Knowing When to Un-Follow People in Real Life

- Recognizing when to disengage from negative or unproductive relationships.

XI. Saying No

- Setting boundaries and making strategic decisions to prioritize your goals.

XII. Good Energy

- Cultivating a positive mindset and outlook in the face of challenges.

XIII. Staying Positive

- Maintaining optimism and resilience throughout your music journey.

XIV. Strategic Partnerships

- Leveraging collaborations and alliances to amplify your impact in the industry.

XV. Making Your Plan B to Make Your Plan A Work

- Developing contingency plans and adaptability strategies for success.

XVI. Music Business Post COVID

- Navigating the changing landscape of the music industry in a post-pandemic world.

XVII. Business Formation

- Understanding legal and organizational considerations for establishing music ventures.

XVIII. Marketing in the Music Business

- Implementing effective strategies to promote and distribute your music.

XIX. Entrepreneurship

- Cultivating an entrepreneurial mindset and approach to your music career.

XX. Protecting and Monetizing

- Safeguarding your creative assets and maximizing revenue opportunities.

XXI. Distribution –

- Exploring channels and platforms for distributing your music to audiences worldwide.

CRAFTING YOUR VISION

The first step towards declaring "MUSIC IS MY BUSINESS" is crafting a vision that's audacious enough to ignite your passion. Your vision should be so colossal that it sends shivers down your spine. If your heart isn't racing at the thought of it, then you're not dreaming big enough. When I ventured into the entertainment industry, I meticulously penned a 5-year plan for my vision. I thought I had it all figured out, but within the first two years, I achieved everything I set out to do. It seemed like a triumph until I realized I hadn't aimed high enough. I had barely scratched the surface of my true potential. If you're going to pursue something, why not strive to be the absolute best at it? True happiness lies in becoming the best version of yourself, not a mere imitation of someone else. It's about unlocking the boundless potential within ourselves. That's why it's imperative to pursue a passion that sets your soul on fire.

SCAN CODE FOR MORE INFO:

GET STARTED

The best way to turn dreams into reality is to take that first step. So, let's dive in! Find a serene spot away from distractions—perhaps a forest, a lakeside, or a tranquil garden. Leave your phone behind; you need time to clear your mind. Sit in quiet contemplation and ask yourself: Why are you embarking on this journey? Envision success in vivid detail and set your sights on achieving it. Arm yourself with pen and paper—no electronics, no interruptions. The first order of business: establishing your brand.

ESTABLISHING A BRAND

WHAT IS A BRAND?

A brand is more than just a logo, slogan, or color scheme. It's the soul of a service or product—a distinct identity, character, and personality. Just like cattle ranchers brand their livestock to distinguish them from others, businesses use branding to set themselves apart from competitors. Brands embody a promise—a commitment to a certain level of quality that customers expect. When someone buys a Coca-Cola, they expect the distinct taste of Coca-Cola—not Pepsi. Similarly, once you establish a brand standard, you're making a promise to your customers. Keeping that promise is essential for retaining their loyalty. At the end of the day, people may not remember product specifics, but they'll never forget the experience your brand delivers.

THE POWER OF EXPERIENCE

It's not just the ingredients but the experience that consumers associate with a brand. A positive experience creates emotional value, fostering customer loyalty and ensuring repeat business. People are creatures of habit; once convinced of the value of your product or service, they become loyal customers for life. Building a brand is not just about selling a product—it's about creating memorable experiences that resonate with consumers long after the transaction is complete.

COMMITTING TO YOUR DREAMS

Commitment to your dreams is non-negotiable. It's about dedicating real time and real effort to see your aspirations come to fruition. Understand that big dreams require ample time and unwavering commitment. Along the way, you'll face challenges and moments of doubt. But quitting is not an option—you owe it to yourself to persevere.

CHEAT CODE: CHOOSE PASSION

You're going to commit to something, no matter what. So why not choose something you love? Too often, people consider quitting when success doesn't come immediately or when obstacles seem insurmountable. Frustration sets in when support or finances are lacking, and impatience grows when results aren't immediate. But comparing your journey to others' is futile. Your path is unique, and patience is key.

THE POWER OF CHOICE

Consider this scenario: Someone decides to abandon their music career for a job they despise—all for the sake of paying bills. In doing so, they prioritize financial obligations over their dreams. They diligently apply for jobs, ace interviews, and eventually land a position. But now, they're bound by rules and routines, committing 8-12 hours a day to a job that drains their passion. And when illness strikes, they're beholden to a boss for time off.

RETHINKING PRIORITIES

As a former manager, I know firsthand that calling in sick isn't always an option. But here's the reality: If you're willing to dedicate countless hours to a job you dislike, why not channel that same energy into pursuing your dreams? It's time to reassess your priorities and commit to the path that ignites your soul.

Commitment is the cornerstone of turning dreams into reality. Whether you're grinding away at a job or pursuing your passion, commitment is essential. Consider this: In a typical job, taking time off requires advance notice and adherence to strict schedules. But here's the catch—commitment to your dreams is no different. Whether you're clocking in at a job you dislike or chasing your dreams, the choice is yours. Your future happiness hinges on this decision. Remember, every action you take today is an investment in your future.

YOU EITHER COMMIT TO YOUR DREAMS OR TO YOUR FEARS. CHOOSE WISELY.

MAKING YOUR PLAN

START: Don't overthink it—just start. Your plan begins with an assessment of your current situation, identifying your goals, strengths, and available resources. Remember, resources aren't just about money; they include your network. As the saying goes, "I never had a dream that I could afford"—the key is to invest in yourself. Your network's net worth determines the extent of your resources. If your network is limited, it's time to hustle and expand it. Connect with people who share your passion and dedication. While not everyone will support you, those who do can open doors to invaluable connections. Cultivate these relationships; they'll pay dividends for years to come.

WHERE DO YOU WANT TO GO?

Success isn't a vague notion—it's a destination. Define what success means to you, write it down, and map out your journey. Don't just aim to "make music"; set clear, tangible goals. Success is personal, so don't assume everyone shares your definition. Just like embarking on a journey without an address, striving for success requires direction. Determine your destination and plot your course accordingly.

ALIGNING WITH YOUR VISION

As you pursue your dreams in the music industry, alignment with your vision is paramount. When your vision aligns with that of others, you'll feel a natural resonance—a sense of connection that signifies you're on the right path. But this alignment only happens when you've put in the work to define what you truly want from music.

NAVIGATING THE JOURNEY

Now, it's time to roll up your sleeves and start working the plan, trusting the process every step of the way. You won't have all the answers at first, and that's perfectly okay. My grandfather, Smokey, imparted a powerful lesson to me as a young man: "Do something even if it's wrong." In other words, take action—even if you're unsure—because most people won't notice, and the rest will appreciate your initiative.

Remember, time is your most precious asset—don't waste it waiting for tomorrow to pursue your dreams. Seize the moment and live your dreams today.

MY PLAN

When I returned to Chicago at 21, fresh from the Army and nursing multiple injuries, I was at a crossroads. The world post-9/11 was tumultuous, and my military career was abruptly cut short. But amid the uncertainty, one thing was clear: my passion for music. So, I decided to marry my love for music with my knack for business.

With little experience and no roadmap, I embarked on a journey to build my own recording studio. It was a bold move for a 21-year-old with a family to support, but I was driven by a relentless determination to make it in the music business. I knew I wouldn't rest until I could proudly proclaim, "MUSIC IS MY BUSINESS."

FLEXIBILITY AND ADAPTABILITY

Developing your plan and brand takes time. Embrace fluidity and allow yourself to flow with the universe. Be flexible, because nothing ever unfolds exactly as planned—especially in the unpredictable realm of the music industry. My journey began with the decision to construct my own studio, but it was just the beginning of a winding path filled with twists and turns.

BUILDING SMOKEY'S STUDIO

When I say "build," I mean literally constructing a recording studio from the ground up. I'm no carpenter or handyman, but I had a vision: to create an in-house studio where I could collaborate with talent on my own terms and build something extraordinary. In 2002, I embarked on the daunting task of bringing Smokey's Studio to life. I found the perfect location—an old loft dating back to 1880, situated above my father's auto repair shop. This historic space, once Al Capone's Beer Depot during Prohibition, held a special allure. It was aged, weathered, and, best of all, free. With sheer determination, perseverance, and the support of loved ones, Smokey's Studio became a reality.

DIVERSIFYING INTO PRODUCTION AND RECORD LABEL

After countless hours of toil, sweat, and financial investments, Smokey's Studio was finally up and running. We wasted no time in collaborating with exceptional talent, leading us to establish a production company and, eventually, a record label. Securing distribution, releasing music, and promoting our artists became our primary focus. At one point, we represented a diverse roster spanning various genres, from Hip-Hop and R&B to Latin Rock, Reggaeton, and beyond. Juggling the responsibilities of running a company while nurturing young talent was no small feat. I wore countless hats—from driver to counselor, producer to roadie. But through it all, my passion for music fueled my drive to succeed.

KEEPING YOUR PLAN SECRET

Keeping your plan under wraps is paramount. Prematurely sharing your ambitions can sabotage your success before it even begins. It's crucial to bide your time, quietly nurturing your vision until it's ready to be unveiled. Actions speak louder than words, so focus on manifesting your dreams rather than broadcasting them prematurely.

Why keep your plan under wraps? Because family and friends, despite their good intentions, can unwittingly crush your dreams. Their own insecurities and societal pressures may lead them to inject doubt into your vision. These are the people closest to you, yet they may not understand or support your aspirations. It's not their fault—they've been conditioned to "play it safe" and may project their fears of failure onto you. Sharing your dreams prematurely can expose them to unnecessary skepticism and negative energy.

COMMITMENT OVER FEAR

Commitment is key—either you commit to progress or succumb to fear. Taking risks, especially in your youth, is essential for growth. Failure is inevitable, but it's also an opportunity to learn and adapt. Remember to learn from others' mistakes as well as your own to avoid repeating them.

FUNDING YOUR BUSINESS

Entertainers often overlook the harsh reality of funding. Money is crucial not only for launching your brand but also for sustaining and expanding your business. There are two options: self-funding or attracting investors. However, the most effective way to attract investors is by first investing in yourself. Putting your own resources into your venture demonstrates your commitment and belief in your brand. It's about showing that you're serious and willing to take risks.

Here's a breakdown of funding options for your music business:

1. **Self-Funding:**
   - Use personal savings, earnings from gigs, or income from other sources to finance your music venture.
   - This option gives you full control over your business and eliminates the need to share profits or decision-making authority with investors.
   - However, it may require significant personal financial investment and could limit the scale of your operations initially.

2. **Attracting Investors:**
   - Investors, such as angel investors or venture capitalists, provide funding in exchange for equity or a stake in your business.
   - To attract investors, you'll need to develop a compelling business plan that outlines your vision, market opportunity, revenue model, and growth strategy.
   - Investors look for businesses with high growth potential and a clear path to profitability, so be prepared to demonstrate how your music business fits these criteria.
   - Networking with industry professionals, attending pitch events, or seeking introductions through mutual connections can help you connect with potential investors.

3. **Crowdfunding:**
   - Crowdfunding platforms like Kickstarter, Indiegogo, or Patreon allow you to raise funds from a large number of people, often in exchange for rewards or perks.
   - This option can be particularly effective for musicians looking to finance specific projects, such as recording an album or producing a music video.
   - Crowdfunding campaigns require careful planning, promotion, and engagement with your fan base to generate interest and support.

4. **Grants and Sponsorships:**
   - Explore opportunities for grants, sponsorships, or subsidies from government agencies, arts organizations, or corporate partners.
   - These sources of funding may be available to support music-related projects, events, or initiatives that align with specific criteria or objectives.
   - Research potential funding opportunities and be prepared to submit proposals or applications that clearly articulate your goals and how you intend to use the funds.

5. **Loans and Lines of Credit:**
   - Consider applying for small business loans or lines of credit from banks, credit unions, or online lenders to finance your music business.
   - Loans require repayment with interest, so it's important to carefully assess your ability to service the debt based on your projected cash flow and revenue.
   - Look for lenders that specialize in working with creative or entertainment businesses and compare terms and rates to find the best option for your needs.

Ultimately, the funding approach you choose will depend on your specific circumstances, goals, and preferences. It's essential to weigh the pros and cons of each option carefully and seek professional advice if needed to make informed decisions about financing your music business.

UTILIZING YOUR NETWORK EFFECTIVELY

Having been independent since a young age, you understand the value of leveraging your network to achieve your goals. Yet, I've found myself guilty of underutilizing this invaluable resource at times. It's a mistake I've learned from, and now I emphasize to my clients the importance of cultivating deeper connections within their existing networks.

BUILDING STRATEGIC PARTNERSHIPS

The key to harnessing the potential of your network lies in developing meaningful relationships. Regularly reaching out to contacts, catching up, and exploring potential collaborations can lead to strategic partnerships. However, it's crucial to assess compatibility: Does their brand align with yours? Do they share your values and goals? Is there genuine chemistry beyond just business? Trust is paramount in partnerships, so take the time to evaluate whether the relationship is worth pursuing.

ACTIVATING YOUR NETWORK

A simple yet effective strategy is to proactively reach out to ten people from your contact list each week. By initiating conversations and following up with messages, you open the door to potential opportunities. Even if the first few attempts don't yield immediate results, persistence pays off. Remember, the worst mistake you can make is failing to follow up. Consistency and reliability are key to building credibility and trust.

THE IMPORTANCE OF FOLLOW-UP

When engaging with new contacts, be diligent in your follow-up efforts. If someone fails to follow through on a request, it's a red flag indicating their lack of commitment. Conversely, those who demonstrate reliability and fulfill their promises earn respect and credibility. I personally assess the seriousness of new contacts by testing their follow-through. Requesting specific information via email and observing their response helps gauge their level of commitment and reliability.

Remember, your reputation hinges on your ability to deliver on your promises. Consistency, reliability, and integrity are the cornerstones of building successful relationships in business and beyond.

INVESTING IN YOURSELF

Investing in yourself is paramount to achieving your dreams. Just as one would invest in education and tools to pursue a career as a barber or mechanic, you must invest in your musical aspirations. Whether it's enrolling in music production courses or purchasing equipment, investing in your craft lays the foundation for success. After all, if you're willing to invest in other professions, why not invest in your passion?

SACRIFICES FOR SUCCESS

Success often requires sacrifice, and my journey in the music business was no exception. Upon returning from the Army, I humbly moved in with my father, trading my independence for the opportunity to pursue my dreams. Sacrifices were made, including sleeping on a sofa bed with my wife and dogs in a small room. However, I viewed these sacrifices as investments in my future. I was determined not to wait for success to come to me—I had to make it happen.

SEIZING OPPORTUNITIES

When faced with the need for additional funds to expand my equipment, I seized an unexpected opportunity. A family friend noticed my dedication to my studio and offered a small loan to help me purchase the necessary equipment. Initially hesitant, I almost missed out on this lifeline due to disbelief. However, I quickly realized the significance of the offer and accepted it, leading to further progress in my journey.

Investing in yourself, making sacrifices, and seizing opportunities are all integral components of achieving success in the music business—or any endeavor, for that matter. By committing to your dreams and believing in yourself, you pave the way for remarkable achievements.

Absolutely, belief in oneself and in one's brand is the cornerstone of success in any venture, especially in the competitive landscape of the music business. When you exude unwavering confidence and passion for your craft, it not only inspires others but also instills trust and credibility in your abilities and vision.

BELIEVE IN YOURSELF

Belief in oneself is non-negotiable on the path to success. It's about having the confidence to pursue your dreams relentlessly, despite any obstacles or doubts that may arise along the way. When you truly believe in your talent, your vision, and your ability to make things happen, others will be drawn to your energy and conviction.

BELIEVE IN YOUR BRAND

Your brand is an extension of yourself—it's what sets you apart, defines your identity, and communicates your values to the world. When you wholeheartedly believe in your brand and what it represents, you radiate authenticity and integrity, which resonates with your audience and attracts supporters, collaborators, and investors.

INSPIRING OTHERS

When your belief in yourself and your brand is unwavering, it becomes infectious. Others can sense your passion and dedication, and it inspires them to believe in you too. Whether it's fans, industry professionals, or potential investors, they're drawn to your authenticity and enthusiasm, and they want to be a part of your journey.

ATTRACTING INVESTORS

Investors are more likely to put their money into something they believe in—something with a passionate, driven individual behind it. When you believe in yourself and your brand wholeheartedly, you create a compelling case for investment. Your confidence and vision convince investors that you're worth betting on, increasing the likelihood of securing the funding you need to take your music business to the next level.

In essence, believing in yourself and your brand isn't just about personal conviction—it's a powerful magnet that attracts opportunities, support, and success. So, embrace your belief, wear it proudly, and watch as it propels you toward your goals in the music business.

BUILDING YOUR SUPREME TEAM

Before delving into the intricacies of assembling your Supreme Team, it's crucial to understand the multifaceted roles they play in the journey of your music business. These individuals are not just colleagues or associates; they are the backbone of your enterprise, the driving force behind your vision, and the custodians of your dreams. From the Alpha Team, comprising your closest confidants and advisors, to the Bravo Team, consisting of dependable collaborators and supporters, each member contributes uniquely to the collective tapestry of your success.

The Alpha Team: Your Inner Circle of Champions

At the core of your Supreme Team lies the Alpha Team, a select group of individuals who share your passion, vision, and unwavering commitment to excellence. These are the people with whom you can sit in a car for 16 hours, engage in heated debates, brainstorm innovative ideas, and weather the storms of uncertainty. They are your trusted allies, your mentors, and your partners in crime.

Selecting the right members for your Alpha Team is a delicate process that requires careful consideration and discernment. Look for individuals who not only possess the requisite skills and expertise but also resonate with your values, ethos, and work ethic. Seek out those who challenge you to elevate your game, inspire you to push past your limits, and empower you to realize your fullest potential.

However, building your Alpha Team is not just about finding seasoned professionals or industry veterans; it's about cultivating meaningful relationships based on mutual respect, trust, and shared aspirations. Sometimes, your most valuable collaborators may be those you least expect—emerging talents, unconventional thinkers, or individuals with diverse backgrounds and perspectives. Keep an open mind and be willing to embrace the unexpected, for greatness often lies beyond the confines of familiarity.

The Bravo Team: Your Network of Champions in Waiting

While the Alpha Team forms the nucleus of your Supreme Team, the Bravo Team comprises the broader network of supporters, collaborators, and fellow travelers on your journey. These are the individuals who may not be intimately involved in your day-to-day operations but play a pivotal role in supporting your endeavors, amplifying your message, and expanding your reach.

Your Bravo Team consists of artists, creators, producers, managers, art directors, editors, interns, and directors—individuals from diverse backgrounds and disciplines who contribute their unique talents and perspectives to your collective vision. While they may not be part of your inner circle, their support and contributions are invaluable in propelling your business forward.

When selecting members for your Bravo Team, focus not only on their skills and qualifications but also on their attitude, mindset, and alignment with your values. Look for individuals who are enthusiastic, proactive, and eager to collaborate, as they will be instrumental in bringing your creative visions to life and executing your strategic initiatives.

Ultimately, building your Supreme Team is an ongoing process of cultivation, refinement, and evolution. It requires patience, perseverance, and a willingness to invest in relationships that transcend transactional exchanges and superficial interactions. By surrounding yourself with the right people—those who share your passion, embody your values, and champion your cause—you can create a synergistic ecosystem of talent, creativity, and collective ambition that propels your music business to new heights of success.

THE FOUR P'S: PAPERWORK, PEOPLE, PROCESS & PRODUCT

PAPERWORK

Paperwork: The Foundation of Business in Music

In the fast-paced world of the music industry, where creativity and collaboration reign supreme, paperwork might not be the most glamorous aspect of the business, but it is undeniably one of the most critical. Properly executed paperwork is the bedrock upon which successful ventures are built, serving as the scaffolding that supports and sustains every aspect of your operations.

Why Paperwork Matters

Paperwork serves several vital functions in the music business, chief among them being clarity, accountability, and legal protection. By documenting agreements, roles, and responsibilities in writing, you establish a clear and unambiguous framework within which all parties operate. This minimizes the risk of misunderstandings, disputes, and conflicts down the line, ensuring smooth collaboration and efficient workflow.

Moreover, in an industry as dynamic and competitive as music, intellectual property is often the most valuable asset you possess. From song lyrics and compositions to audio recordings and brand logos, your intellectual property represents the culmination of your creativity, talent, and hard work. However, without proper safeguards in place, it is vulnerable to exploitation, infringement, and misappropriation.

Key Documents in the Music Business

Understanding the various types of paperwork prevalent in the music industry is essential for safeguarding your interests and maximizing your opportunities for success. Here are some of the key documents you're likely to encounter:

1. **Record Contracts**: Legal agreements between an artist and a record

label outlining the terms of their relationship, including rights to music recordings, royalties, and promotional activities.

2. **Production Agreements**: Contracts between an artist and a producer detailing the production services to be provided, such as recording, mixing, and mastering, as well as compensation and ownership rights.

3. **Split Sheets**: Documents that outline the ownership percentages of songwriters, producers, and other contributors to a musical work, ensuring proper distribution of royalties.

4. **Copyright Registration**: Official registration of original musical compositions with the U.S. Copyright Office to establish legal ownership and protection against unauthorized use.

5. **Non-Disclosure Agreements (NDAs)**: Contracts that protect confidential information shared between parties, commonly used in the music industry for safeguarding unreleased music, business plans, and trade secrets.

6. **Management Contracts**: Agreements between an artist and a manager outlining the manager's responsibilities, compensation, and duration of the partnership.

7. **Distribution Agreements**: Contracts between artists and distributors specifying the terms for distributing and selling music through various platforms, including physical and digital channels.

8. **Performance Contract**: Legal agreements between performers and venues or event organizers detailing the terms of live performances, including fees, dates, and technical requirements.

9. **Release Forms**: Documents signed by individuals granting permission for their likeness, voice, or performance to be used in promotional materials, music videos, or other media.

10. **Licensing Agreement**: Contracts granting permission to use copyrighted music in films, TV shows, commercials, video games, and other media, outlining terms, fees, and usage rights.

11. **Employee Contracts**: Agreements between employers and employees outlining terms of employment, including job responsibilities, compensation, benefits, and termination conditions.

12. **Company Handbooks/Policies**: Documents outlining the rules,

regulations, and expectations for employees within a company or organization, covering topics such as conduct, safety, and procedures.

13. **W2**: Tax forms used by employers to report wages and salaries paid to employees, necessary for filing individual income tax returns.

14. **1099**: Tax forms used to report income earned by independent contractors, freelancers, and self-employed individuals, including musicians and music industry professionals.

15. **Business Name Search**: Research conducted to ensure that a chosen business name is not already in use and is available for registration.

16. **Business Formation LLC/INC.**: Legal documents establishing the formation of a business entity, such as a limited liability company (LLC) or corporation (INC.), including articles of organization or incorporation.

17. **IRS EIN #**: Employer Identification Number issued by the Internal Revenue Service (IRS) for tax identification purposes, required for businesses with employees or multiple owners.

18. **Operating Agreement**: Legal document outlining the ownership and operational structure of a limited liability company (LLC), including management roles, profit sharing, and decision-making processes.

19. **Invoices**: Itemized bills sent by businesses to clients or customers for products sold or services rendered, including details such as quantity, price, and payment terms.

20. **Royalty Registration 12+**: Registration of music royalties with performing rights organizations (PROs) and other entities responsible for collecting and distributing royalty payments to rights holders.

21. **Trademark Registration**: Official registration of trademarks, logos, or brand names with the U.S. Patent and Trademark Office to protect intellectual property and prevent unauthorized use by others.

22. **Contracts**: Legal agreements governing various aspects of the music business, including collaborations, sponsorships, endorsements, and more.

23. **Sync Licenses**: Contracts granting permission to synchronize music with visual media, such as films, TV shows, advertisements, and video

games.

24. **Mechanical Licenses**: Permissions granted by copyright owners to reproduce and distribute copyrighted musical compositions as physical or digital copies, typically for album releases or streaming services.

25. **Performance Rights Organization (PRO) Memberships**: Memberships with organizations such as ASCAP, BMI, or SESAC that collect and distribute performance royalties to songwriters and publishers for public performances of their music.

26. **SoundExchange Registration**: Registration with SoundExchange to collect and distribute digital performance royalties for sound recordings played on digital platforms, satellite radio, and internet radio.

27. **Clearance Agreements**: Contracts securing rights and permissions for the use of copyrighted material, samples, or audiovisual content in music productions to avoid legal disputes.

28. **Merchandising Agreements**: Contracts governing the production, sale, and distribution of merchandise featuring an artist's name, image, or branding, including apparel, accessories, and collectibles.

29. **Venue Contracts**: Agreements between artists and venues outlining terms for live performances, including booking arrangements, technical specifications, and financial agreements.

30. **Tour Rider**: Document specifying the logistical and technical requirements for live performances on tour, including sound, lighting, staging, accommodations, and catering preferences.

31. **Music Publishing Contracts**: Agreements between songwriters and music publishers outlining the administration, exploitation, and monetization of musical compositions, including royalty collection and licensing.

32. **Insurance Policies**: Policies providing coverage for risks and liabilities associated with music-related activities, including equipment insurance, liability insurance, and event cancellation insurance.

33. **Indemnity Agreements**: Contracts shifting liability and responsibility for damages or losses from one party to another,

commonly used to protect against legal claims in the music industry.

34. **Non-Compete Agreements**: Contracts prohibiting employees or business partners from engaging in competitive business for a certain or indefinite amount of time.

PEOPLE

1. **Thinker**: Someone who generates creative ideas, strategies, and solutions for the music business.
2. **Doer**: A proactive individual who executes tasks, projects, and plans effectively and efficiently.
3. **Manager**: An organizer who oversees and coordinates various aspects of the music business, including personnel, operations, and projects.
4. **Engineer**: A skilled technician responsible for recording, mixing, and mastering music in a studio environment.
5. **Leader**: A visionary who provides direction, motivation, and guidance to the team, driving the music business forward.
6. **Financer**: Someone who manages the financial aspects of the music business, including budgeting, investing, and financial planning.
7. **Dreamer**: An individual with big aspirations and long-term goals for the music business, inspiring others with their vision.
8. **Worker**: A dedicated team member who diligently performs tasks and contributes to the overall success of the music business.
9. **Intern**: An entry-level position for individuals gaining experience and learning the ropes of the music industry.
10. **Adviser**: An experienced professional who provides expert advice and guidance on various aspects of the music business.
11. **Consultant**: An external expert hired to provide specialized knowledge and advice on specific projects or challenges.
12. **Lawyer**: A legal expert who handles contracts, intellectual property issues, and legal matters for the music business.
13. **Accountant**: A financial specialist responsible for managing budgets, taxes, payroll, and financial records.
14. **Tech**: A technical expert who handles equipment setup, maintenance, and troubleshooting in the studio or live settings.

15. **Graphic Designer**: An artist who creates visual assets, including album covers, promotional materials, and branding elements.
16. **Mentors**: Experienced professionals who provide guidance, support, and wisdom to individuals navigating the music industry.
17. **Experienced**: Seasoned veterans with years of experience and knowledge in the music business, offering valuable insights and expertise.
18. **Publicist**: A communications specialist responsible for managing publicity, media relations, and press coverage for artists and projects.
19. **Booking Agent**: A representative who secures live performance opportunities, tours, and appearances for artists.
20. **Tour Manager**: An organizer who oversees logistics, scheduling, and operations for touring artists and bands.
21. **Merchandise Manager**: A coordinator responsible for designing, producing, and selling merchandise for artists and tours.
22. **Social Media Manager**: An expert in managing and growing social media accounts, engaging with fans, and promoting content online.
23. **Fan Engagement Coordinator**: Someone who interacts with fans, builds communities, and cultivates relationships to enhance fan engagement.
24. **A&R Representative**: A talent scout responsible for discovering and signing new artists to record labels or management companies.
25. **Sync Licensing Manager**: A specialist who secures placement opportunities for music in film, TV, advertising, and other media.
26. **Studio Manager**: An administrator who oversees the day-to-day operations of a recording studio, including scheduling and client management.
27. **Tour Merchandise Coordinator**: A professional who manages merchandise sales and inventory during live performances and tours.
28. **Marketing Analyst**: A data expert who analyzes market trends, audience behavior, and campaign performance to inform marketing strategies.
29. **Event Coordinator**: An organizer who plans and executes live events, concerts, showcases, and promotional activities.
30. **Music Supervisor**: A specialist who selects and licenses music for use

in film, TV, video games, and other media projects.

31. **Educator/Mentor**: A teacher or mentor who imparts knowledge, skills, and guidance to aspiring individuals in the music industry.

32. **Street Team Leader**: A coordinator who mobilizes grassroots marketing efforts, including street promotions, flyering, and guerrilla marketing tactics.

These roles cover a wide range of responsibilities and expertise required to effectively operate and manage various aspects of a music business, from creative development and promotion to business administration and operations.

SCAN CODE FOR MORE INFO:

PROCESS

Now that you have all your paperwork sorted and the proper people in place working together, we can focus on your process—the engine that drives your business forward. In simple terms, process refers to the series of activities that accomplish specific organizational goals. For your music business, having a clearly defined process is essential. It ensures that you can consistently produce desirable outcomes and replicate your successes.

A well-defined business process offers several benefits. It improves efficiency by eliminating unnecessary steps and optimizing workflows. It also helps identify which tasks are crucial to your business goals, streamlines communication between team members, and facilitates easy troubleshooting when issues arise.

Most importantly, a standardized set of procedures ensures that vital tasks essential to company operations are completed consistently and effectively.

Here's a breakdown of what your business process should entail:

- **Define Your Goals:** Clearly articulate why you're embarking on this journey. Understanding your objectives provides direction and purpose to your efforts.
- **Plan and Map Your Process:** Develop a strategy for success by outlining the steps required to achieve your goals. Mapping out your process helps visualize the workflow and identify potential bottlenecks.
- **Identify and Assign Tasks:** Clearly define each team member's role and responsibilities. Assign tasks based on individual strengths and expertise, setting clear expectations for performance.
- **Test the Process:** Before full implementation, test your process to identify any inefficiencies or areas for improvement. Iteratively refine your workflow to maximize efficiency and effectiveness.
- **Implement the Process:** Once refined, roll out your process across your business operations. Ensure that everyone understands their roles and responsibilities and is equipped to execute their tasks effectively.
- **Monitor the Results:** Continuously monitor and evaluate the results of your process. Document the process history, review performance metrics, and analyze patterns to identify opportunities for further optimization.

By following these steps, you can establish a robust business process that drives your music business forward efficiently and effectively.

PRODUCT

- Hats: Branded headwear, often featuring artist or band logos or designs.

• USB: Custom USB drives containing music, videos, or other digital content.

• Lighters: Custom lighters featuring artist or band logos or designs.

• Posters: Printed posters featuring album artwork, tour dates, or promotional images.

• Air Fresheners: Branded air fresheners featuring scents and designs related to the artist or band.

• Totes: Custom tote bags featuring artist or band logos or designs.

• Notebooks: Branded notebooks or journals featuring artist or band logos or designs.

• Grinders: Custom grinders for herbs or tobacco, featuring artist or band logos or designs.

• Rolling Trays: Custom rolling trays for rolling cigarettes or joints, featuring artist or band logos or designs.

• Patches: Embroidered or printed patches featuring artist or band logos or designs.

• Magnets: Custom magnets featuring artist or band logos or designs.

• Guitar Picks: Custom guitar picks featuring artist or band logos or designs.

• Drumsticks: Custom drumsticks featuring artist or band logos or designs.

• Keychains: Custom keychains featuring artist or band logos or designs.

• Beanies: Branded knit beanies featuring artist or band logos or designs.

• Stickers: Custom stickers featuring artist or band logos or designs.

• Phone Cases: Custom phone cases featuring artist or band logos or designs.

• Earbud Cases: Custom cases for earbuds or headphones featuring artist or band logos or designs.

- Bandanas: Custom bandanas featuring artist or band logos or designs.

- NFTs: Non-fungible tokens representing digital artworks, music, or collectibles.

- Beats: Instrumental tracks available for purchase or licensing.

- Instrumentals: Instrumental versions of songs available for purchase or licensing.

- Background Music – Audio Jungle: Royalty-free background music for various multimedia projects.

- Sample Packs: Collections of audio samples or loops for music production.

- Video Courses: Online courses or tutorials covering various aspects of music production, marketing, or entrepreneurship.

- Software Presets: Preset configurations for music production software or plugins.

- eBooks: Digital books covering topics related to music, business, or self-improvement.

- Mentorship – Via Zoom: One-on-one mentorship sessions with industry professionals conducted via Zoom or other video conferencing platforms.

REVENUE

- Royalties – P.R.O. Performing Rights Organizations: Royalties earned from the performance of music on various platforms and venues, collected by performing rights organizations (P.R.O.s) such as ASCAP, BMI, or SESAC.

- SoundExchange: Royalties earned from the digital performance of sound recordings, collected by SoundExchange.

- Soundscan: Sales tracking service for music sales, providing data used for royalty calculations and chart rankings.

• SongTrust: Music publishing administration service, helping artists and songwriters collect royalties from various sources.

• Mediabase: Music airplay monitoring service used by radio stations and record labels to track song performance.

• Licensing Fees – TV, Film: Fees earned from licensing music for use in television shows, films, commercials, or other media productions.

• Live Performances: Revenue earned from ticket sales, merchandise sales, and other sources during live concerts or performances.

• Fan Subscriptions: Subscription-based services offering exclusive content, merchandise discounts, or other perks to fans in exchange for a recurring fee.

• Video Reels – TikTok, Facebook, Instagram: Revenue earned from monetized video content posted on social media platforms such as TikTok, Facebook, or Instagram.

Each product or service category offers unique opportunities for revenue generation and requires careful management to ensure quality, profitability, and customer satisfaction. Understanding your target audience and market trends is essential for effectively positioning and promoting your products and services in the music industry.

ADDITIONAL REVENUE

• YouTube: Revenue earned from monetized videos on the YouTube platform, including ad revenue, channel memberships, and Super Chat donations.

• Sponsors: Income generated from sponsorship deals with brands or companies, often in exchange for promotion or advertising.

• Music Grants: Funding received from grants or scholarships provided by organizations or institutions to support music projects or endeavors.

• Session Work: Income earned from providing instrumental or vocal performances for recording sessions, often hired by other artists or producers.

• Crowdfunding: Fundraising method where individuals or organizations raise money for projects or ventures by soliciting small contributions from a large number of people, typically via online platforms.

• Distribution: Income generated from distributing music through various channels, such as digital platforms, record stores, or streaming services.

• Streaming – Twitch, YouTube: Revenue earned from streaming live content on platforms like Twitch or YouTube, often through subscriptions, donations, or ad revenue.

• Video Scoring – Commercials, TV Shows, Video Games, Documentaries: Income earned from composing or licensing music for use in various video productions, including commercials, TV shows, video games, and documentaries.

SERVICES

• Audio Engineering: Technical expertise in recording, mixing, and mastering audio content.

• Music Production: The process of overseeing and guiding the creation of musical recordings, from songwriting and arranging to recording and mixing.

• Music Recording: Capturing sound and music performances in a studio or live setting for later reproduction or distribution.

• Music Mixing: Blending individual tracks or elements of a recording to create a balanced and cohesive sound.

• Music Mastering: The final stage of audio production, optimizing the overall sound of a recording for distribution across different formats and platforms.

• Audio Editing: Manipulating and arranging recorded audio material to achieve desired effects or improve clarity and coherence.

• Songwriting: Crafting original compositions, including lyrics and melodies, for use in musical productions.

• Artist Management: Overseeing the career and professional development of musical artists, including booking gigs, negotiating contracts, and managing finances.

• Tour Support: Providing logistical and organizational support for artists during live performance tours, including travel arrangements, equipment setup, and scheduling.

• Music Promotion: Marketing and promoting musical releases or events to increase visibility, attract audiences, and generate sales or attendance.

• Event Promotion: Marketing and promoting live events, such as concerts or festivals, to attract attendees and generate ticket sales.

• Event Sound: Providing sound reinforcement and technical support for live events, ensuring optimal sound quality and coverage for performers and audiences.

WHEN TO UN-FOLLOW IN REAL LIFE

Knowing when to end a professional relationship is crucial for maintaining integrity and efficiency in the music business. Here are some types of individuals you may encounter in your career journey, where ending the professional relationship may be necessary:

Toxic: When a person is toxic to the team environment and always negative, you need to get rid of them ASAP. Negative people will disrupt the positive energy that is necessary to have a productive team. Toxic people will complain and find something wrong no matter what.

Trust: If you cannot trust a person, get rid of them immediately. Don't wait to get burned to trust your gut.

Stagnant: This is more common than most people would think; way too many people are comfortable not progressing. They have found comfort in not progressing in their professional career. They are happy with a routine and do not like to live outside of their comfort level.

Loyalty: If you have to question their loyalty, then you need to remove them from your circle. A lot of people are just loyal to their own needs and what they can get from you. They are not actually loyal to you. If you want to find out if this true, let them get an opportunity to do something else without you and see if they bring you in.

Envy: Envy can be a dangerous weapon, beware of people that want to take what is yours. They will grow jealous and eventually they will betray you.

SAYING NO

Saying No: If you want to be successful in any business, you need to learn to say NO. Too many people overextend themselves trying to please too many people. They don't want to disappoint anyone so they begin to say YES to everything, but then overcommit and complete nothing to their satisfaction because they were spread so thin. You have to know when to say no and when to say yes. You will learn this through trial and error. If you are going to try something, go for it, but if you fail than learn to fail fast so you can move on to your next objective. When to say NO!

Questions to Ask Yourself:

- Does this feel right?

- Is this a good idea?

- Does this align with my values?

- Is this good for my brand?

- Will there be any repercussions?

- Am I excited about this?

- Does this add any value to my life?

- Am I being deceived?

- Do I have more important matters to deal with right now?

- Do I have the time to do this correctly?

- Do I have the energy to do this right now?

- Do I have the resources to do this right now?

How to say NO:

- Just say it.

- I don't have the desire to do this right now.

- I don't think this is a fit for me.

- I have to decline your request right now.

- I don't have any discretion here.

- I simply can't do that.

- I don't feel comfortable doing that.

- Sorry, this is outside of my skillset.

- I am unable to commit to your request.

- My prior commitments prevent me from accepting your offer at this time.

- Thank you for thinking of me, but I cannot fit this in.

When You Should Say NO:

- When you are too busy

- When the cost is too high

- When it's negative

- When it makes you feel uncomfortable

- When you feel guilty or obligated

- When you are overbooked

- When you are sick

- When you are stressed

- When you need to address your mental health

- When you have a set schedule and plan

- When you need to focus on yourself

- When you need to focus on your family

GOOD ENERGY

- Surround yourself with positive people. Seek out those who uplift you, inspire you, and support your goals. Avoid spending time with individuals who drain your energy or bring negativity into your life.

- Practice gratitude daily. Take time to appreciate the good things in your life, no matter how small they may seem. Gratitude helps shift your focus away from negativity and fosters a more positive outlook.

- Focus on solutions rather than problems. When faced with challenges or setbacks, approach them with a mindset of finding solutions. Dwelling on problems only reinforces negativity, while seeking solutions empowers you to overcome obstacles.

- Engage in activities that bring you joy and fulfillment. Whether it's pursuing your passions, spending time in nature, or connecting with loved ones, prioritize activities that uplift your spirits and bring you happiness.

- Cultivate self-awareness and mindfulness. Pay attention to your thoughts, emotions, and energy levels throughout the day. Practice mindfulness techniques such as deep breathing or meditation to center yourself and maintain a positive mindset.

- Practice kindness and compassion towards yourself and others. Treat yourself with the same kindness and understanding that you would extend to a close friend. Show empathy and compassion towards others, recognizing that everyone is fighting their own battles.

By consciously creating and nurturing good energy in your life, you'll not only enhance your own well-being but also contribute to a positive and uplifting environment for those around you.

- Take care of yourself. It's essential to prioritize your physical, mental, and spiritual well-being. Start by being mindful of how you speak to yourself. Your words hold power, so speak to yourself with kindness and positivity. Avoid negative self-talk and instead, affirm yourself with words of encouragement and self-love. Additionally, ensure that your body receives proper rest and nutrition. Limit consumption of fast food and sugary drinks, and prioritize nutritious meals. Regular exercise is crucial for maintaining overall health and reducing stress. Aim to work out 3-5 times a week to keep your body strong and energized. Balancing your mind and body is essential for your spirit. Incorporate activities like meditation, spending time in nature, and disconnecting from electronics to nourish your spirit and find inner peace.

• Keep a gratitude journal. Cultivate a habit of gratitude by keeping a notebook or journal where you write down everything, you're grateful for. Reflect on meaningful aspects of your life and jot them down in your journal regularly. During challenging times, revisit your gratitude list to remind yourself of the blessings in your life. Visualize how different your life would be without those things and appreciate the abundance and goodness that surrounds you. Remember that progress takes time, and practicing gratitude consistently can lead to profound shifts in your perspective and overall happiness

STAYING POSITIVE

Staying positive isn't solely about feeling happy; it's about maintaining composure and professionalism even in challenging situations. It means keeping your cool when someone betrays your trust, staying composed when faced with delays in payment, and reframing setbacks as opportunities for growth. For instance, instead of dwelling on the financial loss from a less profitable event, staying positive involves recognizing the success of hosting a well-executed event without incurring losses.

Your perspective plays a pivotal role in how you perceive and respond to circumstances. By adopting a positive mindset, you can avoid investing unnecessary energy into negative outcomes. Redirecting your focus towards what you want to achieve rather than dwelling on what you don't want can significantly impact your life.

Maintaining a positive outlook offers numerous benefits, including improved energy levels, physical well-being, and psychological health. It can expedite recovery from injuries or illnesses, enhance stress management skills, and even contribute to a longer and more fulfilling life overall. Embracing positivity is a proactive choice that can lead to a better quality of life and greater resilience in the face of adversity.

To stay positive, consider implementing the following strategies:

1. **Don't take yourself too seriously:** Embrace your imperfections and mistakes, and don't let the opinions of others affect your self-worth. Laugh at yourself, learn from your errors, and move forward confidently.
2. **Surround yourself with positive people:** Limit your exposure to negative influences and spend time with individuals who exude positivity and ambition. Positive energy is contagious, and being around like-minded individuals can uplift your spirits and motivate you to pursue your goals.
3. **Maintain a gratitude journal:** Document your journey and

accomplishments, no matter how small they may seem. Reflecting on your past successes and moments of gratitude can remind you of how far you've come and instill confidence during challenging times.

STRATEGIC PARTNERSHIPS

Cultivate strategic partnerships: Be selective about who you collaborate with and ensure that partnerships are mutually beneficial. Focus on forming alliances with individuals or organizations that share your values, vision, and commitment to success.

Choose the right partnerships: Avoid overextending yourself by investing time and resources into partnerships that aren't aligned with your goals or values. Instead, prioritize relationships that offer genuine support, resources, and opportunities for mutual growth.

Remember that commitment and alignment are crucial factors in successful partnerships. By surrounding yourself with positivity, cultivating meaningful relationships, and staying true to your goals, you can maintain a positive mindset and navigate your journey with confidence and resilience.

It's true that in the music industry, as in any other field, people often hold onto relationships for various reasons, even when those relationships may no longer be beneficial or healthy. Loyalty, fear of offending others, and comfort zones can all contribute to this tendency. However, it's important to recognize when these bonds are holding you back from growth and success.

When individuals are toxic, lazy, or unwilling to elevate themselves, it's crucial to reassess the value they bring to your career and artistic journey. Continuing to invest time, energy, and resources into such relationships can ultimately hinder your progress and limit your potential. Loyalty is important, but not at the expense of your own growth and success.

Identifying when a person is not aligned with your goals and future aspirations is the first step. Once you recognize this, it's essential to take decisive action. This may involve having honest conversations with the individual about your concerns and the need to part ways professionally. If cutting ties completely is not possible or desirable, limiting their access to you and redirecting your focus on more important priorities can help maintain boundaries and foster personal growth.

Maintaining laser-like focus on your goals and craft is essential for success in the music industry. This may require temporarily disconnecting from distractions like social media and dedicating yourself wholeheartedly to honing your skills and pursuing your artistic vision. By prioritizing your growth and surrounding yourself with individuals who share your commitment to excellence, you can unlock your full potential and achieve your goals in the music industry.

MAKE YOUR PLAN B TO MAKE YOUR PLAN A WORK

So, I made a decision to fully commit to my passion for music and entrepreneurship. I knew it wouldn't be easy, and I was prepared to face challenges along the way. I understood that success in the music industry requires resilience, determination, and unwavering faith in oneself.

I accepted that I would encounter setbacks and obstacles, but I refused to let them deter me from my ultimate goal. Instead, I saw them as opportunities to learn, grow, and refine my approach. I embraced the mindset of a true professional, someone who takes full ownership of their journey and refuses to settle for mediocrity.

There were sacrifices to be made, both personally and professionally. I had to prioritize my time and resources, often foregoing immediate gratification for the sake of long-term success. I had to be willing to let go of relationships and situations that no longer served my purpose or aligned with my vision.

But through it all, I remained steadfast in my belief in myself and my dreams. I refused to entertain the idea of failure or giving up. I had a singular focus on making my plan A work, knowing that there was no alternative that would bring me the same fulfillment and satisfaction.

And as I persevered through the challenges and embraced the opportunities that came my way, I began to see my hard work pay off. I built a career that I was passionate about, one that allowed me to live authentically and make a positive impact on others.

In the end, it was my unwavering faith in myself and my ability to overcome obstacles that truly separated me from the amateurs. I was willing to do whatever it took to turn my dreams into reality, and that determination ultimately led me to success in the music industry.

In the end, my journey was about more than just pursuing a career in music; it was about reclaiming control over my life and shaping it according to my own terms. I refused to be shackled by the limitations of a traditional job or the whims of others who didn't share my vision.

Instead, I took proactive steps to diversify my income streams and create opportunities for myself. I refused to rely solely on a single source of income that could be taken away from me at any moment. I refused to let others dictate my worth or determine my financial stability.

I was determined to build my own dream, rather than spend my life helping others build theirs. And as I pursued my passion for music and entrepreneurship, I found fulfillment and purpose in every endeavor.

Now, as I reflect on my journey and share my experiences in "MUSIC IS MY BUSINESS: THE ULTIMATE STARTUP GUIDE TO THE MUSIC INDUSTRY," I hope to inspire and empower others who are embarking on their own paths in the music industry.

I hope that my insights and guidance will serve as a beacon of light for those who are navigating the complexities of the music business. May this book be a source of knowledge, advice, direction, and inspiration for all those who dare to dream and strive for success.

Thank you for joining me on this journey, and may you find the courage and determination to make your own dreams a reality.

MUSIC BUSINESS POST-COVID

The COVID-19 pandemic has undoubtedly reshaped the landscape of the music industry, perhaps permanently altering the way artists connect with their audiences and generate revenue. I vividly recall the initial shockwaves felt across the industry as tours were abruptly canceled and venues shuttered their doors. The cancellation of major events like SXSW served as a sobering wake-up call, signaling the severity of the situation.

Fast forward two years, and the repercussions of the pandemic continue to reverberate throughout the music world. The future of live performances appears destined for a significant transformation, with outdoor concerts adopting a drive-in style format and strict capacity limits imposed on indoor venues. Social distancing measures may persist, inhibiting the traditional mingling and interaction between artists and fans.

In response to these challenges, the music industry has increasingly turned to technology as a lifeline. Streaming platforms and virtual concerts have surged in popularity, offering artists alternative avenues to engage with their fan base and monetize their performances. Pay-per-view models are becoming more prevalent, allowing creators to recoup lost revenue from limited-capacity live events.

As we navigate the post-COVID era, it's imperative for artists and industry professionals to embrace technological innovation and adapt to the changing landscape. Those who seize the opportunity to leverage new technologies and creative approaches will likely thrive in this evolving environment. It's a time for forward-thinking individuals to capitalize on emerging trends and carve out their place in the reshaped music industry of tomorrow.

BUSINESS FORMATION

Choosing the right business structure is a critical decision that can have significant legal and tax implications for your company. While I can provide a brief overview, it's essential to consult with a qualified attorney or tax advisor to determine the best option for your specific circumstances.

Here are the most common forms of business entities recognized by the IRS:

1. **Sole Proprietorships**: This is the simplest form of business structure, where the business is owned and operated by one individual. The owner is personally liable for all business debts and obligations.
2. **Partnerships**: A partnership is formed when two or more individuals or entities join together to carry on a business. Partners share in the profits, losses, and liabilities of the business.
3. **Corporations**: Corporations are separate legal entities owned by shareholders. They offer limited liability protection to shareholders, meaning their personal assets are generally not at risk for business debts.
4. **S Corporations**: An S Corporation is a type of corporation that elects to pass corporate income, losses, deductions, and credits through to their shareholders for federal tax purposes. This allows S Corporations to avoid double taxation on corporate income.
5. **Limited Liability Companies** (LLC): An LLC combines the limited liability protection of a corporation with the flexibility and tax advantages of a partnership. LLCs offer personal asset protection to their members while allowing for pass-through taxation.

Each business structure has its own advantages and disadvantages in terms of liability protection, tax treatment, management flexibility, and administrative requirements. Your choice will depend on factors such as the nature of your business, your long-term goals, and your tolerance for risk.

Again, it's highly recommended to consult with legal and tax professionals who can provide personalized advice based on your specific situation and objectives.

SOLE PROPRIETORSHIP

Sole proprietorships offer a straightforward way to operate a business, with the owner having complete control over operations. Here are some key points to consider about sole proprietorships:

1. **Formation**: Sole proprietorships are easy to establish and require no formal registration. If you engage in business activities without registering as any other type of business entity, you are automatically considered a sole proprietor.
2. **Liability**: One significant drawback is that there is no legal separation between the business and the owner's personal assets. As a result, the owner is personally liable for all debts and obligations of the business. This can expose personal assets to risk in the event of lawsuits or financial difficulties.
3. **Business Name**: Sole proprietors can still operate under a trade name, but it does not create a separate legal entity.
4. **Capital**: Raising capital can be challenging for sole proprietors since they cannot sell stock and may face reluctance from banks to extend loans.
5. **Suitability**: Sole proprietorships are often suitable for low-risk businesses or individuals looking to test a business idea before committing to a more formal business structure.
6. **Taxation**: Sole proprietors report business income and expenses on their personal tax return (Form 1040 or 1040-SR) using Schedule C. They are also subject to self-employment tax, which covers Social Security and Medicare contributions. Sole proprietors are responsible for making estimated tax payments throughout the year. Additionally, they must handle employment tax obligations if they have employees, including withholding income tax and paying Social Security and Medicare taxes.
7. **Compliance**: Sole proprietors must fulfill various tax obligations, including filing quarterly or annual tax returns, issuing W-2 forms to employees, and paying federal unemployment tax (FUTA). They may

also need to file information returns for payments to non-employees and transactions with other parties.

Despite the simplicity and flexibility of sole proprietorships, it's essential to weigh the potential risks, especially regarding personal liability, before choosing this business structure. Consulting with a legal or tax professional can provide valuable guidance tailored to your specific circumstances.

PARTNERSHIP

Limited liability partnerships (LLPs) are different in that all partners have some degree of limited liability, shielding them from debts and obligations incurred by the partnership. LLPs are often favored by professional service firms like law or accounting practices.

Here are some key features of partnerships:

1. **Formation**: Partnerships are relatively easy to establish and require a partnership agreement outlining the terms of the partnership, including profit-sharing, decision-making authority, and dispute resolution procedures.

2. **Ownership and Control**: Partnerships allow for shared ownership and decision-making among partners. However, the structure of control and liability varies between limited partnerships and LLPs.

3. **Liability**: In limited partnerships, one partner assumes unlimited liability for the business's debts and obligations (the general partner), while other partners have limited liability. In LLPs, all partners enjoy limited liability protection, shielding their personal assets from business debts and liabilities.

4. **Profit and Loss Sharing**: Partnerships distribute profits and losses according to the terms outlined in the partnership agreement. Typically, profits and losses are allocated based on each partner's contribution to the business or as agreed upon among the partners.

5. **Taxation**: Partnerships are pass-through entities for tax purposes, meaning the business itself does not pay taxes on its income. Instead, profits and losses flow through to the individual partners, who report them on their personal tax returns. Partnerships are required to file an annual information return (Form 1065) to report income, deductions, gains, and losses.

6. **Continuity and Transferability**: Partnerships may face challenges regarding continuity and transferability, as changes in ownership require amendments to the partnership agreement and may trigger dissolution or restructuring.

7. **Management**: Partnerships typically operate under a shared management structure, with partners collectively making decisions regarding business operations, investments, and strategic direction. However, the partnership agreement may designate specific partners with managerial authority or responsibilities.

Partnerships offer a flexible and collaborative approach to business ownership but require careful planning and documentation to address potential challenges and ensure the protection of partners' interests. Consulting with legal and financial professionals is advisable when forming a partnership to navigate legal requirements and establish a solid foundation for the business.

Partnerships indeed offer a versatile structure for businesses with multiple owners or those seeking to explore their business ideas collaboratively. Here's a summary of the key points you've highlighted:

1. **Limited Liability Partnerships (LLPs)**: LLPs provide limited liability protection to all partners, shielding them from the debts and liabilities of the partnership. This differs from limited partnerships where only certain partners have limited liability.
2. **Reporting Partnership Income**: Partnerships must file an annual information return (Form 1065) to report income, deductions, gains, and losses. However, partnerships themselves do not pay income tax. Instead, profits or losses are "passed through" to individual partners, who report them on their personal tax returns using Schedule K-1 (Form 1065).
3. **Employment Taxes**: Partners in a partnership are not considered employees and should not receive Form W-2. Instead, they receive Schedule K-1 to report their share of partnership income. The partnership may have obligations for employment taxes, including Social Security, Medicare taxes, income tax withholding, and federal unemployment (FUTA) tax.
4. **Forms for Partnerships**: Apart from the annual return of income (Form 1065), partnerships may be required to file various forms related to employment taxes, such as Form 941 for quarterly federal tax returns, Form 940 for federal unemployment tax, and other forms for excise taxes.

Understanding the taxation and reporting requirements for partnerships is crucial for maintaining compliance and ensuring proper financial management.

Consulting with tax professionals or legal advisors can provide further guidance tailored to specific business needs and circumstances.

Here's a summary of the forms individuals in partnerships may need to file:

1. **Income Tax Forms**:
    - Form 965-A: Individual Report of Net 965 Tax Liability
    - Schedule E (Form 1040): Supplemental Income and Loss
    - Form 1040: U.S. Individual Income Tax Return or Form 1040-SR: U.S. Tax Return for Seniors

1. **Self-Employment Tax**:
    - Schedule SE (Form 1040): Self-Employment Tax
    - Form 1040: U.S. Individual Income Tax Return or Form 1040-SR: U.S. Tax Return for Seniors

1. **Estimated Tax**:
    - Form 1040-ES: Estimated Tax for Individuals

1. **International Tax Forms**:
    - Form 5471: Information Return of U.S. Persons With Respect to Certain Foreign Corporations and related schedules
    - Form 8082: Notice of Inconsistent Treatment or Administrative Adjustment Request (AAR)
    - Form 8288: U.S. Withholding Tax Return for Dispositions by Foreign Persons of U.S. Real Property Interests
    - Form 8865: Return of U.S. Persons With Respect to Certain Foreign Partnerships

These forms cover various aspects of income tax, self-employment tax, estimated tax payments, and international tax reporting requirements for individuals involved in partnerships. It's important to ensure timely and accurate filing of these forms to comply with tax regulations and avoid potential penalties.

C CORPORATION (C Corp):

- A C corporation is a legal entity separate from its owners, offering strong protection against personal liability.
- Formation of a C corporation involves prospective shareholders exchanging money, property, or both for the corporation's capital stock.
- C corporations are subject to double taxation, where profits are taxed at the corporate level when earned and again at the shareholder level when distributed as dividends.
- However, corporations can take special deductions, and shareholders do not deduct any corporation losses.
- For federal income tax purposes, a C corporation is recognized as a separate tax-paying entity, conducting business, realizing net income or loss, paying taxes, and distributing profits to shareholders.
- C corporations require extensive record-keeping, operational processes, and reporting, with higher formation costs compared to other business structures.

C corporations offer strong protection against personal liability, making them suitable for businesses with medium to higher risk and those planning to raise capital or go public. However, they require more extensive administrative processes and incur double taxation on profits distributed as dividends.

Double Taxation:

- The profit of a C corporation is taxed at the corporate level when earned and again at the shareholder level when distributed as dividends, leading to double taxation.
- The corporation does not receive a tax deduction when distributing dividends to shareholders, and shareholders cannot deduct any losses of the corporation.

Independent Existence:

- C corporations have an independent legal existence separate from their shareholders, allowing them to continue operations relatively undisturbed if a shareholder leaves or sells their shares.

Capital Raising and Stock Sales:

- Corporations have the advantage of raising capital through the sale of stock, which can be beneficial for attracting investors and employees.

Suitability:

- C corporations are suitable for medium- to higher-risk businesses, entities needing to raise significant capital, and those planning to go public or be sold in the future.

Overall, while C corporations offer strong protection against personal liability and are advantageous for raising capital, they entail double taxation and require extensive administrative processes. They are best suited for businesses with growth potential and substantial capital needs.

S CORPORATON (S Corp):

Taxation:

- S corporations, or S corps, are designed to avoid double taxation. Profits and some losses are passed through directly to the owners' personal income without being subject to corporate tax rates.

State Taxation:

- While most states recognize S corporations similarly to the federal government and tax shareholders accordingly, some states may have different regulations. Some states tax S corps on profits above a specified limit, while others treat them as C corporations.

IRS Filing:

- To obtain S corp status, businesses must file with the IRS, following a different process than registering with their state.

Eligibility:

- There are specific eligibility requirements for S corporations, and businesses must adhere to strict filing and operational processes similar to C corporations.

Independent Existence:

- S corporations have an independent legal existence, allowing them to continue operations even if shareholders leave or sell their shares.

Suitability:

- S corporations can be a good choice for businesses that meet the eligibility criteria and want to avoid double taxation. They are particularly suitable for businesses that would otherwise operate as C corporations but meet the requirements to file as an S corp.

Overall, S corporations offer a tax-efficient structure for businesses while maintaining many of the benefits of traditional corporations.

Benefit Corporation (B Corp):

- A B corp is a for-profit corporation recognized in many U.S. states. Unlike traditional C corps, B corps are driven by both profit and mission. Shareholders hold the company accountable to produce public benefits in addition to financial profit. Some states require B corps to submit annual benefit reports demonstrating their contributions to the public good. Third-party certification services exist, but certification is not required for legal recognition as a B corp.

Close Corporation:

- Close corporations have a structure similar to B corps but with fewer formalities. They are typically smaller companies where shares are not publicly traded. Close corporations can be managed by a small group of shareholders without a board of directors.

Nonprofit Corporation:

- Nonprofit corporations are organized for charitable, educational, religious, literary, or scientific purposes. They can receive tax-exempt status, meaning they are not subject to state or federal income taxes on profits. However, nonprofits must file with the IRS to obtain tax-exempt status, following a separate process from state registration.

Nonprofits must adhere to organizational rules similar to those of C corps and have restrictions on profit distribution.

501(c)(3) Corporations:

- Nonprofits are often referred to as 501(c)(3) corporations, named after the section of the Internal Revenue Code granting tax-exempt status.

These different types of corporations offer various structures and benefits to suit the goals and missions of different businesses and organizations.

A Limited Liability Company (LLC)

A Limited Liability Company (LLC) is a popular business structure that combines the limited liability protection of a corporation with the flexibility and tax benefits of a partnership or sole proprietorship. Here's an overview:

Limited Liability Protection:

- The main advantage of an LLC is that it provides limited liability protection to its owners, known as members. This means that the personal assets of members are generally protected from business debts and liabilities. However, there are exceptions, such as personal guarantees or wrongful acts.

Pass-Through Taxation:

- LLCs are generally taxed as pass-through entities, meaning that the profits and losses of the business are passed through to the members' personal tax returns. This avoids double taxation, where both the business and its owners are taxed on the same income.

Flexibility:

- LLCs offer flexibility in management structure and operational procedures. They can be managed either by their members or by appointed managers. Additionally, LLCs have fewer formalities and requirements compared to corporations, making them easier to set up and maintain.

Ownership and Membership:

- LLCs can have one or more members, and ownership interests are typically represented by membership interests. Members can include individuals, corporations, other LLCs, or even foreign entities, depending on state laws.

Operating Agreement:

- While not always required by law, it's advisable for LLCs to have an operating agreement. This document outlines the ownership structure, management responsibilities, voting rights, profit-sharing arrangements, and other important aspects of the business.

State Regulations:

- LLCs are governed by state laws, and the requirements and regulations may vary depending on the state in which the LLC is formed. Generally, forming an LLC involves filing articles of organization with the appropriate state agency and paying the required fees.

Perpetual Existence:

- Unlike sole proprietorships or partnerships, LLCs have perpetual existence, meaning that the business can continue to operate even if one of the members leaves or dies.

Limited Liability Companies Tax Forms:

- LLCs file tax returns using Form 1065 (Partnership Return of Income) if they have more than one member, or they can elect to be taxed as a corporation using Form 8832 (Entity Classification Election).

Overall, LLCs offer a blend of liability protection, tax flexibility, and operational simplicity, making them a popular choice for many small businesses and startups. However, it's essential to consult with legal and tax professionals to understand the specific implications and requirements for your particular situation.

It's crucial to be aware of the specific requirements and regulations imposed by the state in which you plan to operate your business. Each state may have its own set of rules governing business formation, registration, taxation, licensing, permits, and other regulatory matters.

To access information regarding state-level requirements for starting and operating a business, you can visit your state's official website or the website of the Secretary of State's office. These websites typically provide valuable resources, guides, and forms related to business formation and compliance.

Additionally, you may consider seeking assistance from local small business development centers, chambers of commerce, or professional advisors who can offer guidance tailored to your specific location and business needs.

By understanding and adhering to the state-level requirements, you can ensure that your business is compliant with applicable laws and regulations, setting a solid foundation for its success.

BUSINESS PLAN

Writing a business plan for the music business follows a similar structure to that of other industries, but it includes specific elements tailored to the music industry's unique characteristics and challenges. Here's a comprehensive guide on how to write a business plan for the music business:

1. **Executive Summary:**
   - Provide a brief overview of your music business, including its mission statement, goals, and key highlights.
   - Summarize your business concept, target market, products/services offered, and competitive advantages.
   - Highlight key financial projections and funding requirements.

2. **Business Description:**
   - Provide detailed information about your music business, including its name, legal structure (e.g., sole proprietorship, LLC, corporation), location, and history (if applicable).
   - Describe the products or services you offer, such as music production, recording, distribution, live performances, merchandising, etc.
   - Explain your unique selling proposition (USP) and how your business stands out from competitors.

3. **Market Analysis:**
   - Conduct market research to analyze the music industry landscape, including trends, demographics, target audience preferences, and market size.
   - Identify your target market segments, such as music consumers, artists, event organizers, record labels, etc.
   - Assess the competitive landscape, including existing music businesses, their strengths, weaknesses, opportunities, and

threats (SWOT analysis).

4. **Organization and Management:**
   - Outline the organizational structure of your music business, including key personnel, roles, and responsibilities.
   - Provide bios of the management team, highlighting their relevant experience and expertise in the music industry.
   - Describe any strategic partnerships or collaborations with artists, producers, distributors, or other stakeholders.

5. **Marketing and Sales Strategy:**
   - Define your marketing strategy to promote your music business and attract customers.
   - Identify your target audience and outline your plans for reaching and engaging them through various marketing channels, such as social media, websites, concerts, events, etc.
   - Detail your sales strategy, including pricing, distribution channels, sales promotions, and customer acquisition tactics.

6. **Product and Service Line:**
   - Describe your music products or services in detail, including their features, benefits, and pricing.
   - Explain how your products/services meet the needs and preferences of your target market.
   - Highlight any unique or innovative aspects of your offerings that differentiate them from competitors.

7. **Funding Request:**
   - Estimate your startup costs and ongoing expenses, including equipment, studio rental, marketing, personnel, etc.
   - Specify the amount of funding you need to launch or expand your music business and how you plan to utilize the funds.
   - Provide financial projections, including revenue forecasts, profit margins, cash flow statements, and break-even analysis.

8. **Financial Projections:**
   - Prepare detailed financial projections for the next three to five years, including income statements, balance sheets, and

cash flow statements.

- Include assumptions underlying your financial forecasts and sensitivity analysis to assess the impact of changes in key variables.

9. **Appendices:**
    - Include any additional supporting documents, such as resumes of key personnel, contracts, legal documents, market research data, and other relevant materials.

Remember to tailor your business plan to your specific music business model, target market, and goals. Regularly review and update your business plan as your music business evolves and market conditions change. Additionally, seek feedback from industry experts, mentors, or advisors to ensure your business plan is comprehensive and realistic.

START-UP COSTS

Starting a career in the music business involves various startup expenses that aspiring musicians, producers, promoters, or other industry professionals need to consider. Here are some common startup expenses:

1. **Equipment and Instruments:**
    - Musical instruments (e.g., guitars, keyboards, drums)
    - Studio equipment (e.g., microphones, audio interfaces, speakers)
    - Recording software and hardware
    - Music production tools (e.g., MIDI controllers, synthesizers)

2. **Studio Space:**
    - Renting or leasing a recording studio or rehearsal space
    - Acoustic treatment and soundproofing materials
    - Equipment and furniture installation and setup costs

1. **Education and Training:**

- Music lessons or workshops to improve skills
- Courses or certifications in music production, sound engineering, or music business management
- Music theory books or online resources

2. **Marketing and Promotion:**
   - Designing and printing promotional materials (e.g., flyers, business cards)
   - Creating a professional website or portfolio
   - Social media marketing tools and advertising budget
   - Press kits and demo CDs for promotional purposes

3. **Legal and Administrative Costs:**
   - Registering a business entity (e.g., LLC, sole proprietorship)
   - Obtaining licenses or permits for music distribution, performances, or events
   - Consulting fees for legal advice on contracts, copyrights, and intellectual property rights
   - Accounting software or services to manage finances and taxes

4. **Networking and Industry Events:**
   - Attending music conferences, workshops, or networking events
   - Membership fees for industry associations or organizations
   - Travel and accommodation expenses for attending industry events or meetings

5. **Merchandise and Merchandising:**
   - Designing and producing merchandise (e.g., T-shirts, hats, posters)
   - Manufacturing costs for CDs, vinyl records, or digital downloads
   - Inventory management software or services for merchandising operations

6. **Performance and Touring Costs:**
   - Booking fees for performance venues or concert halls
   - Travel expenses for touring (e.g., transportation, accommodations)

- Hiring session musicians or backup performers for live shows

7. **Insurance and Risk Management:**
    - Liability insurance for performances, events, or studio operations
    - Equipment insurance to protect against loss, theft, or damage
    - Health insurance for self-employed musicians or industry professionals

8. **Miscellaneous Expenses:**
    - Office supplies and equipment (e.g., computers, printers, stationery)
    - Utility bills and internet expenses for home-based studios or offices
    - Professional development and training resources
    - Emergency fund for unexpected expenses or setbacks

It's essential to create a detailed budget and prioritize expenses based on your immediate needs and long-term goals. Consider seeking advice from industry professionals or financial advisors to plan your startup expenses effectively and ensure a successful launch in the music business.

HOW TO ESTABLISH BUSINESS CREDIT

Establishing business credit in the music business is crucial for accessing financing, securing favorable terms with suppliers, and building a strong financial reputation. Here are steps to help you establish business credit:

1. **Incorporate Your Business:**
   - Choose a legal structure such as a corporation (C-corp or S-corp), limited liability company (LLC), or partnership.
   - Register your business entity with the appropriate state authorities and obtain a Federal Employer Identification Number (FEIN) from the IRS.

2. **Open a Business Bank Account:**
   - Separate your personal and business finances by opening a dedicated business bank account.
   - Use your business bank account for all business-related transactions, including deposits, payments, and expenses.

3. **Obtain Necessary Licenses and Permits:**
   - Ensure your music business complies with all applicable federal, state, and local regulations.
   - Obtain any required licenses or permits for operating your business legally.

4. **Establish a Business Address and Phone Number:**
   - Use a physical business address (not a PO box) and a professional business phone number for your company.
   - This helps legitimize your business and makes it easier for lenders and suppliers to verify your identity.

5. **Apply for a Business Credit Card:**
   - Apply for a business credit card in your company's name.
   - Use the business credit card for business-related expenses and make timely payments to build a positive credit history.

6. **Establish Trade Credit Relationships:**
   - Establish trade credit relationships with suppliers, vendors, and service providers.

- Start by working with companies that report payment history to business credit bureaus.

7. **Pay Your Bills on Time:**
   - Pay all your business bills and invoices on time or ahead of schedule.
   - Timely payments demonstrate creditworthiness and help build a positive credit profile.

8. **Monitor Your Business Credit Report:**
   - Regularly monitor your business credit report from major business credit bureaus such as Dun & Bradstreet, Experian, and Equifax.
   - Check for inaccuracies and dispute any errors promptly to maintain an accurate credit profile.

9. **Establish a Track Record:**
   - Build a solid track record of responsible financial management and credit usage over time.
   - Consistently demonstrate your ability to manage credit and repay debts to strengthen your business credit profile.

10. **Seek Financing When Needed:**
    - Once you have established business credit, consider applying for financing options such as business loans, lines of credit, or equipment financing.
    - Use credit responsibly and avoid overextending your business's financial resources.

By following these steps and managing your business finances effectively, you can establish and maintain a strong business credit profile in the music industry. This will enable your music business to access financing, negotiate better terms with suppliers, and position itself for long-term success.

HOW TO GET VENTURE CAPITAL FUNDING

How to secure venture capital funding specifically for businesses within the music industry:

1. **Understand the Music Industry Landscape:**

- Before seeking venture capital, it's essential to have a thorough understanding of the music industry, including its various sectors such as music production, distribution, live events, streaming platforms, technology, and artist management.
- Identify emerging trends, challenges, and opportunities within the music industry that your business aims to address or capitalize on.

2. **Define Your Niche and Value Proposition:**
   - Clearly define your niche within the music industry and articulate your unique value proposition. Whether you're developing innovative music technology, launching a new record label, or creating a music-focused e-commerce platform, emphasize what sets your business apart from competitors.
   - Highlight how your business addresses a specific need or pain point within the music ecosystem and the potential impact it could have on the industry.

3. **Validate Your Business Concept:**
   - Conduct market research to validate the demand for your music-related product or service. Gather feedback from musicians, industry professionals, potential customers, and other stakeholders to assess market fit and refine your business concept.
   - Provide evidence of market validation, such as customer surveys, pilot programs, or early adopter testimonials, to demonstrate the viability of your business idea to investors.

4. **Assemble a Strong Team:**
   - Investors place a significant emphasis on the strength and expertise of the founding team. Build a team with diverse skill sets and industry experience relevant to your music business.
   - Highlight the credentials, track record, and domain expertise of your team members in music production, technology, business development, marketing, and finance.

1. **Create a Detailed Financial Plan:**
   - Develop a comprehensive financial plan that outlines your revenue projections, cost structure, pricing strategy, and funding requirements.
   - Provide realistic financial forecasts and assumptions based on thorough market analysis and industry benchmarks. Investors will scrutinize your financial projections to assess the potential return on investment.

2. **Seek Music Industry-Specific Investors:**
   - Identify venture capital firms, angel investors, and corporate venture arms with a focus on the music industry. Look for investors who have a deep understanding of the music business landscape and a track record of funding successful music startups.
   - Attend music industry conferences, pitch events, and networking gatherings to connect with potential investors and advisors with expertise in the music sector.

3. **Leverage Music Industry Partnerships:**
   - Forge strategic partnerships with established players in the music industry, such as record labels, streaming platforms, music publishers, and artist management agencies.
   - Collaborating with industry partners not only validates your business model but also enhances your credibility and attractiveness to investors who value industry connections and endorsements.

4. **Highlight Intellectual Property and Innovation:**
   - If your music business involves proprietary technology, patents, or intellectual property (IP), emphasize the innovative aspects of your product or service.
   - Highlight any competitive advantages, technological innovations, or disruptive features that differentiate your offering and create barriers to entry for potential competitors.

5. **Prepare a Compelling Pitch Deck:**
   - Develop a compelling pitch deck tailored to music industry

investors, highlighting the unique value proposition, market opportunity, competitive landscape, growth potential, and financial projections of your business.

○ Use visuals, case studies, and real world examples to illustrate your business concept and its potential impact on the music industry.

6. **Navigate Due Diligence and Negotiations:**
   ○ Be prepared for rigorous due diligence from potential investors, including legal, financial, and operational assessments of your music business.
   ○ Negotiate investment terms, valuation, equity ownership, board representation, and exit strategies with investors to ensure alignment of interests and mutual understanding of expectations.

7. **Execute and Scale Responsibly:**
   ○ Once you secure venture capital funding, focus on executing your business plan, achieving key milestones, and delivering on your promises to investors.
   ○ Prioritize sustainable growth, customer acquisition, product development, and market expansion while managing resources efficiently and responsibly.

By following these steps and tailoring your approach to the unique characteristics of the music industry, you can enhance your chances of securing venture capital funding for your music business venture.

CHOOSE YOUR BUSINESS NAME

Choosing the right business name is a crucial step in establishing your brand identity and attracting customers. Here's a guide to help you choose and protect your business name effectively:

1. **Brainstorm Business Name Ideas:**
   ○ Start by brainstorming a list of potential business names that resonate with your brand identity, values, and target audience.

- Consider the uniqueness, memorability, and relevance of each name idea. Avoid generic or overly complex names that may be difficult for customers to remember or spell.

2. **Conduct Market Research:**
   - Once you have a list of name ideas, conduct market research to ensure that the names are not already in use by competitors or trademarked by other businesses.
   - Check online directories, social media platforms, domain name availability, and trademark databases to verify the availability of your chosen business name.

3. **Evaluate Brand Consistency:**
   - Ensure that the chosen business name aligns with your brand identity, mission, and values. It should convey the essence of your business and resonate with your target audience.
   - Consider how the business name will be perceived across different marketing channels, including your website, social media profiles, and promotional materials.

4. **Legal Considerations:**
   - Understand the legal requirements and implications of registering and protecting your business name. Different registration methods offer varying levels of legal protection and may be required based on your business structure and location.
   - Consult with legal professionals or business advisors to determine the most appropriate registration options for your business.

5. **Register Your Business Name:**
   - Choose the most suitable method(s) to register your business name based on your specific needs and legal obligations:
     - **Entity Name Registration:** Register your business name at the state level to establish legal recognition and protection within your operating jurisdiction.
     - **Trademark Registration:** Consider registering your business name as a trademark at the federal level to obtain exclusive rights to use the name in commerce and prevent others from

using it.

- **Doing Business As (DBA) Registration:** If operating under a name different from your legal entity's name, file a DBA registration to inform the public of your business name and comply with local regulations.
- **Domain Name Registration:** Secure a domain name that matches your business name to establish an online presence and prevent others from acquiring a similar web address.

6. **Protect Your Brand Identity:**
   - Once registered, actively monitor and protect your business name and brand identity from infringement, unauthorized use, and misrepresentation.
   - Enforce your legal rights and take appropriate action against any infringements or violations of your trademark or business name rights.

By following these steps and conducting thorough research and legal due diligence, you can choose and protect a business name that strengthens your brand identity and sets you up for success in the marketplace.

REGISTER WITH STATE AGENCIES

To register your music business with state agencies, especially if it's an LLC, corporation, partnership, or nonprofit corporation, follow these steps:

1. **Determine State Registration Requirements:**
   - Research the specific registration requirements for your business structure in each state where you conduct business activities.
   - Consider factors such as physical presence, revenue sources, and employee locations to determine if registration is necessary in a particular state.
2. **Choose a Registered Agent:**
   - Select a registered agent who will receive official documents and legal notices on behalf of your music business.
   - The registered agent must have a physical address in the state

where you register your business and be available during regular business hours to accept service of process.

- ○ You may choose to appoint yourself as the registered agent, but many businesses opt to use professional registered agent services for convenience and compliance.

3. **Complete Registration Forms:**
   - ○ Obtain the required registration forms from the Secretary of State's office, Business Bureau, or Business Agency in each state where you need to register.
   - ○ Fill out the registration forms accurately and completely, providing information about your business entity, ownership structure, registered agent, and principal place of business.

4. **Submit Registration Documents:**
   - ○ Depending on the state's requirements, you may be able to register online, or you may need to file paper documents in person or by mail.
   - ○ Pay any applicable filing fees associated with the registration process. Fees vary by state and business structure.

5. **Stay Compliant with Ongoing Requirements:**
   - ○ After registering your music business, ensure compliance with any ongoing filing and reporting requirements imposed by the state.
   - ○ Stay informed about renewal deadlines, annual reports, and other obligations to maintain your business's good standing with state agencies.

6. **Consider Using Professional Services:**
   - ○ If you're unfamiliar with the registration process or prefer assistance, consider using professional services such as registered agent services or business filing companies.
   - ○ These services can streamline the registration process, provide guidance on compliance matters, and help ensure that your business meets all legal requirements.

By following these steps and fulfilling the necessary registration obligations in each state where you conduct business activities, you can properly register your music business with state agencies and operate in compliance with state laws and regulations.

FILE FOREIGN QUALIFICATION

To file for foreign qualification for your music business, follow these steps:

1. **Determine Foreign Qualification Requirements:**
   - If your music business operates in multiple states, you may need to file for foreign qualification in states other than your state of formation.
   - Research the foreign qualification requirements in each state where your business is active to understand the necessary steps and obligations.
2. **Prepare Required Documents:**
   - Obtain the appropriate forms for foreign qualification from the Secretary of State's office or equivalent agency in each state where you need to file.
   - Gather necessary information such as your business name, location, ownership details, management structure, registered agent information, and, if applicable, the number and value of shares.
3. **Obtain a Certificate of Good Standing:**
   - Some states may require a Certificate of Good Standing (also known as a Certificate of Existence or Certificate of Authorization) from your state of formation to demonstrate that your business is in good standing.
   - Request the Certificate of Good Standing from the Secretary of State's office or equivalent agency in your state of formation.
4. **File for Foreign Qualification:**
   - Complete the foreign qualification application or Certificate of Authority form for each state where you need to register as a foreign entity.
   - Include any required supporting documents, such as the

      Certificate of Good Standing and filing fees, with each application.

- Submit the applications and fees to the appropriate state agencies either online, by mail, or in person, following the instructions provided by each state.

5. **Pay Filing Fees:**
   - Each state charges a filing fee for foreign qualification, and the amount varies depending on the state and your business structure.
   - Ensure that you include the correct filing fees with each application, and be prepared to pay any additional fees that may apply.

6. **Stay Compliant with Ongoing Requirements:**
   - Once your music business is foreign qualified in other states, comply with any ongoing filing and reporting requirements imposed by those states.
   - Stay informed about renewal deadlines, annual reports, and other obligations to maintain your business's foreign qualification status and good standing in each state.

By following these steps and fulfilling the necessary foreign qualification requirements in states where your music business operates, you can ensure compliance with state laws and continue conducting business activities legally across multiple jurisdictions.

GET FEDERAL AND STATE TAX ID NUMBERS

To obtain federal and state tax ID numbers for your music business, follow these steps:

Federal Tax ID Number (EIN)

1. **Determine Need for an EIN:**
   - If your music business pays employees, operates as a corporation or partnership, files tax returns for certain types of taxes, withholds taxes on non-wage income to non-

resident aliens, uses a Keogh Plan, or engages with specific types of organizations, you'll need an Employer Identification Number (EIN).

2. **Apply for an EIN:**
   - Use the IRS online EIN Assistant tool to apply for your EIN.
   - Provide necessary information such as your name, Social Security Number (SSN), address, and your "doing business as" (DBA) name.
   - Once you complete the application, your nine-digit federal tax ID (EIN) will be available immediately upon verification.

3. **Record Your EIN:**
   - Keep your EIN in a secure location, as you'll need it for various business transactions and tax filings.

4. **Change or Replace Your EIN (If Necessary):**
   - If your business undergoes certain changes such as a name change, address change, changes in ownership or management, or changes in tax status, you may need to change or replace your EIN.
   - Check with the IRS to determine whether a change or replacement of your EIN is necessary based on your specific circumstances.

State Tax ID Number

1. **Research State Requirements:**
   - Determine whether your state requires a separate state tax ID number for your music business.
   - Check with your state's department of revenue or taxation for specific requirements and procedures.

1. **Apply for a State Tax ID Number:**
   - If your state requires a separate tax ID number, follow the procedures outlined by your state's department of revenue or

taxation.
- Submit any required forms and information to obtain your state tax ID number.

2. **Record Your State Tax ID Number:**
- Keep a record of your state tax ID number in a secure location alongside your federal EIN.

By obtaining both federal and state tax ID numbers for your music business, you ensure compliance with tax laws and facilitate various business transactions, including hiring employees, opening bank accounts, and filing tax returns.

SETTING UP YOUR BUSINESS BANK ACCOUNT:

1. **Choose the Right Bank:**
- Research different banks and their business account offerings.
- Consider factors such as fees, account features, branch locations, online banking options, and customer service.

2. **Gather Required Documents:**
- Check with your chosen bank to find out which documents are needed to open a business account.
- Commonly required documents include:
  - Business license or registration certificate
  - Employer Identification Number (EIN)
  - Business formation documents (e.g., articles of organization/incorporation)
  - Personal identification (e.g., driver's license, passport) for each business owner or authorized signer

3. **Visit the Bank or Apply Online:**
- Schedule an appointment with a business banker at your chosen bank branch, or apply online if the option is available.
- Complete the application form with accurate information

about your business.

4. **Deposit Funds:**
   - Once your account is approved, deposit the initial funds required to open the account. This amount varies depending on the bank and the type of business account.

5. **Choose the Right Account Type:**
   - Select the type of business account that best suits your needs, such as a checking account, savings account, or money market account.
   - Consider additional services offered by the bank, such as business credit cards, merchant services, and online banking tools.

6. **Set Up Online Banking:**
   - Register for online banking to manage your account remotely, access account statements, transfer funds, and perform other banking tasks.

1. **Order Checks and Debit Cards:**
   - Order business checks and debit cards to make payments and withdrawals for your business transactions.

2. **Establish Account Signatories:**
   - Determine who will have access to the account and be authorized to sign checks and make transactions.
   - Ensure that appropriate internal controls are in place to safeguard against unauthorized access and fraud.

3. **Review and Maintain Account:**
   - Regularly review your account statements and monitor transactions to ensure accuracy and detect any unauthorized activity.
   - Keep your business account in good standing by maintaining the required minimum balance and promptly addressing any issues or concerns.

By setting up a dedicated business bank account for your music business, you can streamline your financial management, maintain accurate records, and demonstrate professionalism in your business dealings.

MERCHANT SERVICES ACCOUNT

Opening a merchant services account is crucial for businesses, including those in the music industry, as it allows you to accept various forms of electronic payments, such as credit and debit cards. Here are some important factors to consider when opening a merchant service account for your music business:

1. **Types of Accepted Payments:**
   - Ensure that the merchant services provider supports the types of payments your business needs, including major credit cards, debit cards, mobile payments (e.g., Apple Pay, Google Pay), and online payments.
2. **Transaction Fees:**
   - Understand the fee structure associated with the merchant account, including transaction fees, processing fees, monthly fees, statement fees, and any other applicable charges. Compare fees across different providers to find the most cost-effective option for your business.
3. **Contract Terms and Length:**
   - Review the terms of the merchant services agreement carefully, including contract length, cancellation fees, and any early termination penalties. Opt for providers with flexible terms and no long-term commitments if possible.
4. **Payment Processing Equipment:**
   - Determine what type of payment processing equipment you need for your business, such as point-of-sale (POS) terminals, mobile card readers, virtual terminals for online payments, or payment gateway integration for e-commerce websites.
5. **Security and Compliance:**
   - Ensure that the merchant services provider complies with

Payment Card Industry Data Security Standard (PCI DSS) requirements to safeguard sensitive cardholder data and protect against fraud. Look for features like encryption, tokenization, and EMV chip card technology.

6. **Integration with Business Systems:**
   - If your music business uses specific software or platforms for sales, inventory management, or accounting, choose a merchant services provider that offers seamless integration with these systems to streamline operations and reporting.

7. **Customer Support and Service:**
   - Evaluate the quality of customer support provided by the merchant services provider, including availability, responsiveness, and technical assistance. Look for providers with dedicated support teams and multiple channels of communication.

8. **Risk Management and Underwriting:**
   - Understand the underwriting process and risk management practices of the merchant services provider, especially if your music business is considered high-risk due to factors like irregular sales volume, chargeback rates, or industry-specific risks.

9. **Scalability and Growth Potential:**
   - Choose a merchant services provider that can accommodate the growth and expansion of your music business, offering scalable solutions, higher processing volumes, and additional services as your business evolves.

10. **Reputation and Reviews:**
    - Research the reputation and reviews of potential merchant services providers online, considering factors like reliability, transparency, and overall customer satisfaction. Seek recommendations from other businesses in the music industry.

By carefully considering these factors and selecting the right merchant services provider for your music business, you can ensure smooth payment processing, enhanced security, and improved customer satisfaction.

BUSINESS INSURANCE

In the music business, like any other industry, having the right insurance coverage is crucial to protect your assets, mitigate risks, and ensure the continuity of your operations. Here are some types of business insurance that you should consider for your music business:

1. **General Liability Insurance:**
    - General liability insurance provides coverage for third-party bodily injury, property damage, and advertising injury claims. It protects your business from liabilities arising from accidents, slips and falls, or negligence claims. This coverage is essential for music venues, studios, event organizers, and other businesses that interact with the public.
2. **Property Insurance:**
    - Property insurance covers physical assets such as buildings, equipment, instruments, and inventory against risks like fire, theft, vandalism, and natural disasters. It helps your music business recover from property damage or loss and ensures that you can replace or repair essential assets.

1. **Equipment Insurance:**
    - Equipment insurance, also known as inland marine insurance or musical instrument insurance, protects your musical instruments, sound equipment, recording gear, and other specialized equipment used in your business. It provides coverage for theft, damage, loss, and accidental breakage, both on and off-premises.
2. **Commercial Auto Insurance:**
    - If your music business owns or operates vehicles for business purposes, such as transporting equipment, delivering goods, or traveling to gigs, you'll need commercial auto insurance.

This coverage protects your vehicles and drivers against accidents, property damage, bodily injury, and other liabilities.

3. **Professional Liability Insurance (Errors and Omissions Insurance):**
    - Professional liability insurance, also known as errors and omissions (E&O) insurance, provides coverage for claims of professional negligence, errors, or omissions that result in financial losses for clients. It's essential for music producers, agents, promoters, and other professionals who provide services or advice to clients.

4. **Workers' Compensation Insurance:**
    - Workers' compensation insurance is required for businesses with employees and provides coverage for medical expenses, lost wages, and disability benefits for employees who suffer work-related injuries or illnesses. It's crucial for music venues, studios, event organizers, and businesses with production crews or staff.

5. **Cyber Liability Insurance:**
    - Cyber liability insurance protects your music business from financial losses and liabilities associated with data breaches, cyberattacks, and other cyber threats. It covers expenses such as data recovery, notification costs, legal fees, and regulatory fines resulting from a cyber incident.

6. **Event Cancellation Insurance:**
    - Event cancellation insurance provides coverage for financial losses incurred due to the cancellation, postponement, or interruption of concerts, festivals, tours, or other music events due to unforeseen circumstances such as adverse weather, natural disasters, or artist cancellations.

7. **Business Interruption Insurance:**
    - Business interruption insurance, also known as business income insurance, compensates your music business for lost income and operating expenses if you're forced to suspend operations due to covered perils such as property damage or

loss. It helps you maintain financial stability during the recovery period.

8. **Copyright Infringement Insurance:**
    - Copyright infringement insurance provides coverage for legal expenses and damages resulting from claims of copyright infringement, unauthorized use of copyrighted material, or intellectual property disputes. It's essential for music publishers, labels, distributors, and other businesses involved in music licensing and distribution.

Before purchasing insurance coverage for your music business, assess your specific risks, consult with an insurance agent or broker specializing in commercial insurance for the music industry, and tailor your coverage to meet your unique needs and budget. Regularly review and update your insurance policies as your business grows and evolves to ensure adequate protection against emerging risks.

BUYING BUSINESS INSURANCE

Buying business insurance for your music business involves several steps to ensure you get the right coverage tailored to your specific needs. Here are the steps to follow:

1. **Assess Your Risks:**
    - Identify the potential risks and liabilities associated with your music business. Consider factors such as the type of services you provide, the equipment you use, the venues you operate in, and the number of employees you have. Assessing your risks will help you determine the types and levels of coverage you need.
2. **Research Insurance Providers:**
    - Research insurance providers that specialize in providing coverage for the music industry. Look for insurers with experience working with music venues, studios, event organizers, musicians, producers, and other professionals in the music business. Compare the types of coverage offered,

customer reviews, financial stability, and reputation of each provider.

3. **Understand Insurance Coverage:**
   - Familiarize yourself with the different types of business insurance coverage available for the music industry, such as general liability, property insurance, equipment insurance, professional liability, and cyber liability insurance. Understand what each type of coverage includes, its limits, exclusions, and any additional riders or endorsements you may need.

4. **Get Multiple Quotes:**
   - Request quotes from several insurance providers to compare rates and coverage options. Provide accurate information about your music business, including its size, location, operations, revenue, and any specific risks or liabilities you want to insure against. Compare the quotes to find the best value for your insurance needs.

5. **Customize Your Coverage:**
   - Work with an insurance agent or broker specializing in commercial insurance for the music industry to customize your coverage based on your unique risks and budget. Tailor your insurance policy to include the specific types and levels of coverage you need, as well as any additional endorsements or riders to enhance your protection.

6. **Review Policy Terms and Conditions:**
   - Carefully review the terms and conditions of the insurance policies offered, including coverage limits, deductibles, premiums, exclusions, and any endorsements or riders. Make sure you understand what is covered and what is not covered by each policy to avoid surprises in the event of a claim.

7. **Purchase Insurance Policies:**
   - Once you've selected the insurance policies that meet your needs, complete the application process and purchase the policies from the chosen insurance provider. Review the policy documents, payment terms, and cancellation policies

before signing any contracts or making payments.

8. **Maintain and Update Coverage:**
    - Regularly review and update your insurance coverage as your music business grows and evolves. Notify your insurance provider of any changes to your operations, equipment, locations, or staffing levels that may affect your insurance needs. Stay informed about emerging risks and new insurance products available in the music industry.

9. **Keep Records and Documents:**
    - Keep detailed records of your insurance policies, premiums, payments, claims, and correspondence with your insurance provider. Store important documents in a secure location and make digital copies for easy access. Be prepared to provide documentation in the event of a claim or audit.

10. **Work with a Trusted Advisor:**
    - Consider working with an experienced insurance agent or broker who understands the unique risks and challenges faced by music businesses. A knowledgeable advisor can help you navigate the insurance buying process, assess your risks, and find the right coverage solutions to protect your business effectively.

By following these steps and working with trusted insurance professionals, you can purchase comprehensive business insurance coverage for your music business and safeguard your assets, reputation, and financial stability against unforeseen risks and liabilities.

MANAGE YOUR FINANCES

Managing finances in the music business is crucial for the success and sustainability of your career. Here are some tips to help you effectively manage your finances:

1. **Create a Budget:**
    - Establish a budget that outlines your income and expenses. Include revenue streams such as music sales, performance

fees, merchandise sales, royalties, and other sources of income. Track your expenses, including production costs, equipment purchases or rentals, marketing and promotion, touring expenses, and overhead costs like rent and utilities. Having a budget will help you track your financial performance and make informed decisions about spending and investments.

2. **Separate Personal and Business Finances:**
   - Open separate bank accounts for your personal finances and your music business. Keeping your finances separate makes it easier to track business income and expenses, maintain accurate records for tax purposes, and assess the financial health of your music career.

3. **Track Your Income and Expenses:**
   - Keep detailed records of your income and expenses using accounting software or spreadsheets. Track every dollar you earn and spend, including payments received, invoices issued, receipts for purchases, and business-related transactions. Regularly review your financial records to monitor cash flow, identify trends, and make adjustments to your budget as needed.

4. **Manage Cash Flow:**
   - Monitor your cash flow to ensure you have enough funds to cover your expenses and financial obligations. Anticipate seasonal fluctuations in income, such as higher earnings during peak touring seasons or album releases, and plan accordingly. Consider setting aside a cash reserve or emergency fund to cover unexpected expenses or periods of lower income.

5. **Minimize Expenses:**
   - Look for opportunities to reduce unnecessary expenses and optimize your spending. Negotiate better deals with suppliers, vendors, and service providers. Consider sharing resources with other musicians or collaborating on projects to save money. Evaluate the return on investment for each

expense and prioritize spending on activities that generate the highest value and impact for your music career.

6. **Diversify Income Streams:**
   - Explore multiple revenue streams to diversify your income and reduce reliance on any single source of revenue. In addition to music sales and live performances, consider alternative income streams such as merchandise sales, licensing and sync opportunities, crowdfunding campaigns, teaching music lessons, digital streaming royalties, sponsorships, and endorsements.

7. **Save and Invest Wisely:**
   - Set aside a portion of your income for savings and investments to build long-term financial security. Establish short-term savings goals for emergencies, major purchases, or upcoming projects, as well as long-term savings goals for retirement or future career opportunities. Consider working with a financial advisor to develop a personalized savings and investment strategy based on your financial goals and risk tolerance.

8. **Plan for Taxes:**
   - Stay informed about tax obligations and deadlines applicable to your music business. Keep accurate records of your income, expenses, and deductions to prepare for tax filing season. Consult with a tax professional or accountant to ensure compliance with tax laws, maximize deductions, and minimize tax liability. Consider setting aside funds throughout the year for estimated tax payments to avoid surprises at tax time.

9. **Monitor and Evaluate Performance:**
   - Regularly review your financial performance and key performance indicators (KPIs) to assess the health and progress of your music business. Analyze metrics such as revenue growth, profit margins, return on investment (ROI), and cash flow trends. Identify areas of strength and areas for improvement, and adjust your financial strategies

and tactics accordingly to achieve your goals.

10. **Seek Professional Advice:**
	- Consider seeking advice from financial professionals, such as accountants, bookkeepers, or financial advisors, who specialize in working with musicians and music businesses. They can provide valuable guidance, expertise, and support to help you make informed financial decisions and optimize your financial management practices.

By implementing these financial management strategies and practices, you can effectively manage your finances in the music business, achieve your financial goals, and build a sustainable and successful music career.

HIRE AND MANAGE EMPLOYEES AND CONTRACTORS

Hiring and managing employees and contractors in the music business requires careful planning, effective communication, and adherence to legal and ethical guidelines. Here are some steps to help you hire and manage personnel effectively:

1. **Define Roles and Responsibilities:**
	- Clearly define the roles and responsibilities of each position within your music business. Determine the skills, qualifications, and experience required for each role, whether it's a permanent employee or a contractor. Develop job descriptions outlining key duties, performance expectations, and reporting structures.
2. **Recruit Talent:**
	- Use a variety of recruitment methods to attract talent, including online job boards, social media platforms, industry networks, and referrals. Tailor your recruitment strategies to the specific needs and requirements of each position. Conduct interviews to assess candidates' qualifications, skills, cultural fit, and passion for music.
3. **Provide Clear Contracts and Agreements:**
	- Create clear and comprehensive contracts or agreements for

employees and contractors outlining terms of employment, compensation, work expectations, confidentiality agreements, intellectual property rights, termination procedures, and any other relevant terms and conditions. Ensure that all parties understand and agree to the terms before commencing work.

4. **Comply with Employment Laws:**
   - Familiarize yourself with relevant employment laws, regulations, and labor standards applicable to your jurisdiction. Ensure compliance with laws governing wages, working hours, overtime pay, employee benefits, anti-discrimination, harassment prevention, workplace safety, and other legal requirements. Seek legal advice if necessary to ensure compliance with complex regulations.

5. **Establish Effective Communication Channels:**
   - Foster open and transparent communication channels between management, employees, and contractors. Establish regular team meetings, one-on-one check-ins, and feedback sessions to discuss goals, performance expectations, project updates, and any concerns or feedback. Encourage a culture of collaboration, respect, and mutual support within your music business.

6. **Provide Training and Development Opportunities:**
   - Invest in training and development programs to enhance the skills, knowledge, and professional growth of your employees and contractors. Offer opportunities for continuing education, workshops, seminars, and skill-building initiatives relevant to their roles and career aspirations. Support career advancement and skill diversification to retain top talent and foster loyalty.

7. **Offer Competitive Compensation and Benefits:**
   - Provide competitive compensation packages and benefits to attract and retain talented individuals in the music industry. Consider offering salary or hourly wages, performance-based bonuses, health insurance, retirement plans, paid time off,

flexible work arrangements, and other perks or incentives tailored to the needs and preferences of your workforce.

8. **Promote a Positive Work Culture:**
   - Cultivate a positive and inclusive work culture that values diversity, creativity, innovation, and collaboration. Foster a supportive and empowering environment where employees and contractors feel valued, motivated, and engaged. Recognize and celebrate achievements, milestones, and contributions to boost morale and team spirit.

9. **Address Performance Issues Promptly:**
   - Address performance issues, conflicts, or misconduct promptly and professionally through constructive feedback, coaching, and disciplinary actions if necessary. Provide opportunities for improvement and set clear expectations for behavior and performance standards. Document performance evaluations, feedback sessions, and disciplinary actions for record-keeping and accountability.

10. **Promote Work-Life Balance:**
    - Encourage and support work-life balance initiatives to promote employee well-being, productivity, and satisfaction. Offer flexible work arrangements, telecommuting options, wellness programs, and resources for stress management, mental health support, and work-life integration. Respect boundaries and encourage employees to prioritize self-care and personal time outside of work.

By following these steps and best practices, you can effectively hire and manage employees and contractors in the music business, build a talented and motivated team, and create a positive and productive work environment conducive to success and growth.

DIFFERENCE BETWEEN EMPLOYEES AND CONTRACTORS

Understanding the difference between an employee and a contractor is crucial for business owners to ensure compliance with employment laws, tax regulations, and other legal requirements. Here are the key distinctions between an employee and a contractor:

1. **Nature of Work Relationship:**
   - **Employee:** An employee typically works under the direction and control of the employer. The employer has the authority to dictate how, when, and where the work is performed. Employees often receive training, use company equipment, and are integral to the ongoing operations of the business.
   - **Contractor:** A contractor, also known as an independent contractor or freelancer, operates as a separate business entity and provides services to the client under a contract or agreement. Contractors have more independence and autonomy in how they perform the work and are responsible for managing their own business operations.

2. **Control and Supervision:**
   - **Employee:** Employers have significant control over employees, including the ability to direct and supervise their work, set schedules, provide guidance, and evaluate performance. Employers may also provide tools, equipment, and resources necessary to perform the job.
   - **Contractor:** Contractors have more control over their work processes and methods. They typically set their own hours, use their own tools and equipment, and determine how to complete the work according to the terms of the contract. Contractors may work for multiple clients simultaneously and have greater flexibility in managing their workload.

3. **Employment Benefits and Protections:**
   - **Employee:** Employees are entitled to various employment benefits and protections under labor laws, including minimum wage, overtime pay, unemployment insurance, workers' compensation, health insurance, retirement benefits, and other statutory benefits. Employers are

responsible for withholding taxes from employee wages and contributing to payroll taxes on behalf of employees.

- **Contractor:** Contractors are not entitled to employee benefits or protections since they are considered self-employed individuals or separate businesses. Contractors are responsible for paying their own taxes, obtaining their own insurance coverage, and managing their own business expenses. They are generally not eligible for unemployment benefits or workers' compensation from the client.

4. **Duration and Permanence of Relationship:**
   - **Employee:** Employment relationships are typically ongoing and indefinite, with the expectation of continuous work and long-term commitment from both parties. Employees may have employment contracts specifying terms of employment, but the relationship is generally intended to be stable and enduring.
   - **Contractor:** Contractor relationships are often project-based or temporary, with defined start and end dates specified in the contract. Contractors may work on a specific project or assignment for a limited duration, after which the contract may be renewed or terminated based on the client's needs. Contractors have the flexibility to work for multiple clients on different projects.

5. **Legal Classification and Tax Treatment:**
   - **Employee:** Employees are classified as W-2 workers for tax purposes, and employers are responsible for withholding income taxes, Social Security, and Medicare taxes from employee wages. Employers must also contribute to unemployment insurance and pay employer payroll taxes on behalf of employees.
   - **Contractor:** Contractors are classified as 1099 workers for tax purposes, and clients are not required to withhold taxes from contractor payments. Contractors are responsible for

reporting their income and paying self-employment taxes, including income tax, Social Security, and Medicare taxes, directly to the IRS. Clients must issue Form 1099 to contractors for tax reporting purposes if payments exceed a certain threshold.

It's important for businesses to correctly classify workers as employees or contractors to avoid potential legal and financial liabilities. Misclassification of workers can result in penalties, fines, back taxes, and legal disputes with regulatory agencies. If there is uncertainty about the classification of a worker, businesses should seek guidance from legal counsel or consult with tax professionals to ensure compliance with applicable laws and regulations.

MARKETING IN THE MUSIC BUSINESS

Marketing in the music business is essential for promoting artists, their music, and their brand to a target audience. It involves various strategies and tactics aimed at increasing awareness, generating interest, and ultimately driving sales or streams of music. Here's an overview of marketing in the music industry and how artists can effectively market themselves:

1. **Understanding Your Audience:**
    - Identify your target audience based on demographics, psychographics, and music preferences.
    - Understand their behaviors, preferences, and where they consume music (e.g., streaming platforms, social media, live events).

2. **Developing Your Brand:**
    - Define your unique brand identity, including your music style, image, message, and values.
    - Create a compelling story that resonates with your audience and sets you apart from other artists.
    - Establish a consistent visual identity across your artwork, merchandise, social media profiles, and website.

3. **Creating Quality Music:**
    - Focus on creating high-quality music that showcases your talent, creativity, and authenticity.
    - Produce professionally recorded tracks with polished production and engaging lyrics.
    - Experiment with different genres, styles, and collaborations to broaden your appeal and reach new audiences.

4. **Building an Online Presence:**
    - Create a professional website and social media profiles to showcase your music, upcoming events, and behind-the-scenes content.
    - Regularly update your profiles with new music releases, videos, photos, and engaging posts to keep your audience

engaged.

- Use social media platforms like Instagram, Facebook, Twitter, TikTok, and YouTube to connect with fans, share updates, and build relationships.

5. **Utilizing Digital Marketing:**
   - Use digital marketing tactics such as search engine optimization (SEO), email marketing, and online advertising to reach a wider audience.
   - Optimize your website and social media profiles for search engines to improve visibility and attract organic traffic.
   - Build an email list of fans and subscribers to send regular updates, exclusive content, and promotional offers.

6. **Engaging with Your Audience:**
   - Interact with fans and followers through comments, messages, and live streams to foster a sense of community and loyalty.
   - Encourage user-generated content by sharing fan covers, remixes, and fan art on your social media profiles.
   - Offer exclusive perks and rewards to your most dedicated fans, such as VIP access to events, merchandise discounts, and private concerts.

7. **Networking and Collaborating:**
   - Collaborate with other artists, producers, and influencers to expand your reach and tap into new fan bases.
   - Attend industry events, music conferences, and networking mixers to connect with industry professionals, potential collaborators, and media outlets.
   - Build relationships with music bloggers, journalists, radio DJs, and playlist curators to secure coverage and airplay for your music.

8. **Promoting Your Music:**
   - Release singles, EPs, albums, and music videos on digital platforms like Spotify, Apple Music, SoundCloud, and YouTube.
   - Plan strategic release dates, promotional campaigns, and

> marketing initiatives to maximize exposure and impact.
> - Submit your music to online music blogs, playlists, and streaming platforms to increase visibility and attract new listeners.

By implementing these marketing strategies and tactics, artists can effectively promote themselves and their music in the competitive music industry, build a loyal fan base, and advance their careers.

These are excellent steps to enhance your digital marketing efforts in the music business:

1. **Build a Strong Online Presence:** Utilize major social media platforms like Instagram, Facebook, Twitter, and YouTube to connect with your audience. Engage with your fans regularly by sharing behind-the-scenes content, music updates, and interactive posts. Additionally, explore short-form music-driven apps like TikTok and Snapchat to reach a younger demographic.
2. **Create an Electronic Press Kit (EPK):** Develop a comprehensive EPK that showcases your music, bio, press releases, photos, videos, and upcoming gigs. This professional package will help you pitch yourself to industry influencers such as record labels, agents, producers, and venue bookers.
3. **Design a Website:** Establish a dedicated artist or band website where fans can discover your music catalog, tour dates, bio, discography, merch shop, and links to your social channels and email list. Regularly update your website with fresh content to keep fans engaged and informed about your latest releases and activities.
4. **Utilize Digital Distribution Platforms:** Distribute your music and videos to streaming platforms like Spotify, Apple Music, and YouTube through digital distribution services. Ensure that you have the necessary rights to your music before distributing it. Opt for reputable distribution options that offer fair terms and transparent pricing, avoiding those that require monthly fees that can become burdensome.

By implementing these strategies, you can effectively leverage digital marketing to expand your reach, engage with your audience, and promote your music in the competitive music industry.

EMAIL MARKETING

Email marketing is a powerful tool for engaging with your fans and promoting your music career. Here are some key steps to effectively utilize email marketing:

1. **Build Your Email List:** Start by collecting email addresses from your current network, including fans, industry professionals, music critics, bloggers, DJs, and more. Utilize sign-up forms on your website, collect business cards at events, and use in-person sign-up sheets at live shows. Offer incentives such as merch discounts or exclusive access to encourage sign-ups.

2. **Choose an Email Marketing Service:** Select an email marketing service provider that offers features such as list management, customizable templates, automation, and analytics. Popular options include Mailchimp, Constant Contact, and ConvertKit.

3. **Segment Your Audience:** Divide your email list into segments based on factors such as location, music preferences, engagement level, or purchase history. This allows you to send targeted and relevant content to different groups of subscribers.

4. **Create Compelling Content:** Craft engaging and personalized email content that resonates with your audience. Share updates about new releases, upcoming shows, merchandise drops, meet-and-greet opportunities, and behind-the-scenes insights. Use eye-catching visuals, compelling subject lines, and clear calls-to-action to encourage interaction.

5. **Maintain Consistency:** Establish a regular email schedule, whether it's weekly, bi-weekly, or monthly, to keep your audience informed and engaged. Consistency helps build anticipation and loyalty among your subscribers.

6. **Measure and Analyze Performance:** Monitor key metrics such as

open rates, click-through rates, and conversion rates to assess the effectiveness of your email campaigns. Use this data to refine your strategies and optimize future campaigns for better results.

7. **Comply with Regulations:** Ensure that your email marketing practices comply with relevant regulations such as the CAN-SPAM Act. Obtain consent from subscribers before sending them marketing emails, provide an option to unsubscribe, and include your contact information in every email.

By following these steps, you can effectively leverage email marketing to nurture relationships with your fans, promote your music, and grow your music career.

SCAN CODE FOR MORE INFO:

MUSIC BLOGS

Pitching yourself to music blogs is a strategic way to gain exposure and attract new fans to your music. Here's how you can effectively pitch yourself to music blogs:

1. Research Blogs: Take the time to research music blogs that align with your genre and style. Look for blogs that feature artists similar to you and have a track record of promoting independent or emerging musicians.

2. Personalize Your Pitch: Craft a personalized pitch for each blog you reach out to. Address the blogger by name if possible and mention specific articles or features on their blog that you enjoyed. Show that you've done your homework and genuinely appreciate their work.

3. Keep It Concise: Keep your pitch short, sweet, and to the point. Highlight the most important information about yourself, such as

your latest releases, upcoming shows, or significant achievements. Include links to your music, social media profiles, and press kit for easy access.

4. Be Professional: Approach your pitch with a professional demeanor. Use proper grammar and spelling, and avoid sounding overly promotional or desperate. Remember that bloggers receive numerous pitches every day, so standing out with professionalism can make a difference.

5. Include High-Quality Assets: Attach high-quality assets to your pitch, such as professional press photos, music files, streaming links, and a short artist bio. Make it easy for the blogger to listen to your music and visualize your brand.

6. Consider Paid Opportunities: Some music blogs offer paid submission options for artists looking to gain priority placement or additional promotion. While not necessary, investing in these opportunities can sometimes yield valuable exposure and networking opportunities.

7. Follow Up: If you don't hear back from a blogger after your initial pitch, don't be afraid to follow up politely after a week or two. Keep your follow-up brief and friendly, and express your continued interest in being featured on their blog.

By following these tips, you can increase your chances of successfully pitching yourself to music blogs and getting your music heard by new audiences.

PLAYLIST CURATORS

Connecting with playlist curators is an essential strategy for promoting your music and reaching a wider audience on streaming platforms. Here's how you can effectively connect with playlist curators in the music business:

1. Identify Relevant Playlists: Start by identifying playlists that align with your genre, style, and target audience. Look for playlists on streaming platforms like Spotify, Apple Music, and Deezer that feature similar artists or music that fits your sound.

2. Research Curators: Once you've identified relevant playlists, research

the curators or creators behind them. Many playlists are curated by individual users, influencers, or music industry professionals. Look for contact information or social media profiles where you can reach out to them.

3. Engage on Social Media: Follow playlist curators on social media platforms like Twitter, Instagram, and LinkedIn. Engage with their content by liking, commenting, and sharing posts related to music. Building a genuine connection and showing support for their work can increase your chances of getting noticed.

4. Personalize Your Outreach: When reaching out to playlist curators, personalize your messages to show that you've done your research and genuinely appreciate their playlists. Mention specific tracks or playlists that you enjoy and explain why you think your music would be a good fit.

5. Provide High-Quality Music: Make sure your music is of high quality and ready for playlist placement. Provide streaming links to your tracks on platforms like Spotify, Apple Music, or SoundCloud, making it easy for curators to listen and consider adding your music to their playlists.

6. Offer Incentives: Consider offering incentives to playlist curators to encourage them to feature your music. This could include exclusive content, early access to new releases, or promotional opportunities for their own brand or playlist.

7. Submit through Official Channels: Some streaming platforms have official submission processes for artists looking to get their music on playlists. Follow these guidelines and submit your music directly through official channels whenever possible.

8. Be Persistent but Polite: Understand that playlist curators receive numerous submissions and may not respond to every message. Be persistent in your outreach efforts, but always remain polite and respectful. Avoid spamming or bombarding curators with multiple messages.

By following these tips and strategies, you can effectively connect with playlist curators in the music business and increase your chances of getting your music featured on popular playlists, ultimately reaching a larger audience and gaining exposure for your music.

PLAY LIVE SHOWS

Performing live shows is a crucial aspect of building your music career and connecting with your audience. Here are some key points to consider when playing live shows:

1. **Refine Your Performance**: Live shows provide an opportunity to refine your performance skills, stage presence, and interaction with the audience. Pay attention to crowd reactions and adjust your performance accordingly to engage the audience effectively.
2. **Gain Experience**: Especially in the beginning stages of your music career, you may perform at smaller venues or alongside other independent artists. Use these opportunities to gain valuable experience, build your confidence on stage, and learn from other musicians.
3. **Connect with Your Audience**: Live shows offer a unique opportunity to connect with your audience on a personal level. Take the time to interact with the crowd, share stories behind your songs, and make them feel involved in the performance.
4. **Receive Feedback**: Live performances provide immediate feedback from the audience, allowing you to gauge their reactions to your music. Pay attention to audience responses, applause, and energy levels to understand what resonates with them and what areas you can improve upon.
5. **Networking Opportunities**: Live shows also serve as valuable networking opportunities where you can connect with other musicians, industry professionals, and potential fans. Be open to collaborations, exchange contact information, and build relationships within the music community.
6. **Promote Your Music**: Use live shows as a platform to promote your music, merchandise, and upcoming releases. Encourage audience members to follow you on social media, sign up for your mailing list,

and support your music through purchases and streaming.

7. **Stay Professional**: While performing live is an exciting experience, it's essential to remain professional at all times. Arrive early for soundchecks, adhere to venue rules and schedules, and conduct yourself professionally on stage and off.

Overall, live shows play a vital role in the growth and success of your music career. Embrace every opportunity to perform live, engage with your audience, and showcase your talent as a musician.

MUSIC VIDEOS

The visual element of music, especially through music videos, is crucial for engaging with your audience and enhancing the overall experience of your music. My business Urban Grind TV created significant revenue from producing music videos early in my career. Here are some key points to consider when creating music videos:

1. **Quality Over Quantity**: As you mentioned, it's better to focus on producing high-quality music videos that resonate with your audience rather than churning out numerous low-quality videos. A single impactful visual can leave a lasting impression and garner more attention than multiple mediocre videos.

2. **Creative Concept**: Take the time to develop a creative concept for your music video that complements the theme and message of your song. Brainstorm ideas that are visually captivating, memorable, and align with your artistic vision.

3. **Budget Considerations**: While high-budget music videos can be impressive, you don't necessarily need to spend a fortune to create compelling visuals. It's possible to achieve great results on a modest budget by collaborating with talented videographers, editors, and production teams who are passionate about bringing your vision to life.

4. **Collaboration**: Work with professionals who share your passion and vision for the project. Collaborate with videographers, directors, and editors who understand your music and can translate it into visually

stunning content. Their expertise and creativity can elevate the quality of your music video.

5. **Attention to Detail**: Pay attention to every aspect of the production process, including cinematography, editing, visual effects, and storytelling. Ensure that every frame reflects the mood, tone, and emotion of your music, creating a cohesive and immersive viewing experience for your audience.

6. **Promotion and Distribution**: Once your music video is ready, focus on promoting it across various platforms to reach a wider audience. Utilize social media, video streaming platforms, and music blogs to share your video and engage with your fans. Encourage viewers to like, comment, share, and subscribe to your channel to increase visibility. Take advantage of our music video distribution that we offer at UrbanGrindTV.com

By prioritizing quality, creativity, and collaboration, you can create music videos that not only enhance your music but also establish a strong visual identity and connection with your audience.

DISTRIBUTE YOUR MUSIC VIDEO

Distributing your music video effectively is crucial for reaching a wider audience and maximizing its impact. Here are some steps to consider when distributing your music video in the music business:

1. **Choose Distribution Platforms**: Identify the platforms where you want to distribute your music video. This may include popular video streaming platforms like YouTube, Vimeo, Vevo, and Dailymotion, as well as social media platforms such as Facebook, Instagram, and Twitter.

2. **Upload to Video Streaming Platforms**: Create accounts on relevant video streaming platforms and upload your music video. Optimize your video title, description, and tags with relevant keywords to improve visibility and searchability. Consider creating a visually appealing thumbnail that captures viewers' attention.

3. **Share on Social Media**: Leverage your social media channels to

promote your music video. Share teaser clips, behind-the-scenes footage, or still images from the video to generate excitement and anticipation among your followers. Encourage fans to like, comment, share, and tag their friends to increase engagement. A lot of artists leverage the "going live" tactic to show their fans in real time the process.

4. **Collaborate with Influencers**: Partner with influencers, content creators, and music bloggers in your niche to help promote your music video. Reach out to individuals or channels with a large following and ask if they'd be interested in sharing your video with their audience in exchange for promotion or compensation. The influencers will be smaller at first but you can build up as you create more influence and strategic partnerships.

5. **Email Marketing**: Utilize your email list to notify subscribers about the release of your music video. Craft a compelling email campaign with a catchy subject line, engaging content, and a clear call-to-action directing recipients to watch the video. Consider offering exclusive content or incentives to subscribers to encourage them to watch and share the video.

6. **Submit to Music Blogs and Websites**: Research music blogs, online magazines, and websites that feature music videos in your genre. Submit your music video for consideration and include a press release, artist bio, and relevant links. Getting featured on reputable music blogs can help increase exposure and credibility. Sometimes it can be worth sponsoring the post, especially around release time. My company Urban Grind TV provides blog packages that provide placement on multiple blogs at UrbanGrindTV.com.

7. **Pitch to Playlist Curators**: Identify playlists on streaming platforms that feature music videos similar to yours. Reach out to playlist curators and submit your video for consideration. Provide a brief introduction, along with a link to your video and any relevant information about your music and artistic vision. This is another time when having a marketing budget for placement will help expedite the process. Entrepreneurs can often use the placement on a bigger playlist to help pitch smaller playlist curators.

8. **Engage with Your Audience**: Monitor the performance of your music video across different platforms and engage with your audience. Respond to comments, messages, and feedback from viewers to foster a sense of community and connection. Encourage fans to share their thoughts and experiences related to the video.

By strategically distributing your music video across various channels and engaging with your audience, you can increase visibility, generate buzz, and grow your fan base in the music business.

SCAN CODE FOR MORE INFO:

ENTREPRENUERSHIP

Entrepreneurship in the music business involves applying business principles and strategies to navigate the complexities of the music industry, create opportunities, and build successful careers. Here are some key aspects of entrepreneurship in the music business:

1. **Identifying Opportunities**: Entrepreneurs in the music industry are adept at recognizing emerging trends, gaps in the market, and new opportunities for innovation. This could involve identifying underserved audiences, developing unique music concepts, or leveraging new technologies for music creation, distribution, and promotion. Keep track of these opportunities in your notes with details. When entrepreneurs communicate with people, they should write down notes in their phone/notepad for the follow-up conversation. These notes will keep the entrepreneur organized and efficient.

2. **Business Planning**: Like any entrepreneurial endeavor, success in the music business often requires careful planning and strategizing. This includes setting clear goals, defining target audiences, budgeting resources, and developing a roadmap for achieving objectives. A well-thought-out business plan can help guide decision-making and mitigate risks.

3. **Building a Brand**: Establishing a strong personal brand or brand identity is essential for musicians and music entrepreneurs. This involves cultivating a unique artistic persona, developing a distinct visual style, and creating a consistent narrative that resonates with fans and industry stakeholders. A compelling brand can help differentiate artists from competitors and attract loyal followers.

4. **Monetization Strategies**: Entrepreneurs in the music industry must explore various monetization strategies to generate revenue from their music and creative endeavors. This may include selling music recordings, merchandise, concert tickets, licensing music for films, TV shows, and commercials, as well as leveraging digital platforms

for streaming and royalties.

5. **Networking and Relationship Building**: Building strong relationships with industry professionals, collaborators, fans, and influencers is critical for success in the music business. Networking opportunities abound at music events, conferences, festivals, and online platforms. Cultivating genuine connections can lead to valuable partnerships, collaborations, and opportunities for exposure. Networking can play a tremendous role in any entrepreneur's career in the entertainment industry.

6. **Adaptability and Innovation**: The music industry is constantly evolving, driven by changes in technology, consumer preferences, and market dynamics. Successful music entrepreneurs are adaptable and innovative, willing to embrace new trends, experiment with different approaches, and pivot when necessary to stay relevant and competitive. When entrepreneurs fail to adapt in the music business, they quickly fall behind others that have not only adapted to but have leveraged the new technology.

7. **Marketing and Promotion**: Effective marketing and promotion are essential for building awareness, expanding reach, and attracting audiences in the music industry. This may involve developing comprehensive marketing campaigns, leveraging social media and digital platforms, securing press coverage, and engaging in grassroots promotion efforts.

8. **Financial Management**: Music entrepreneurs must possess basic financial literacy and effectively manage their finances to sustain their careers. This includes budgeting for recording costs, touring expenses, marketing campaigns, and other operational expenses, as well as tracking revenue streams, royalties, and taxes. This can become a daunting task if entrepreneurs do not become organized and implement systems for their business.

9. **Continuous Learning and Growth**: The music industry is dynamic and ever-changing, requiring music entrepreneurs to continuously learn, adapt, and grow. This may involve staying abreast of industry trends, attending workshops and seminars, seeking mentorship from experienced professionals, and investing in ongoing education and

skill development.

Overall, entrepreneurship in the music business requires a combination of creativity, business acumen, resilience, and strategic thinking. By embracing entrepreneurial principles and leveraging opportunities, music entrepreneurs can build sustainable careers and make meaningful contributions to the music industry.

MY STORY

During my college years, I held a job in the railroad industry as an Operations Manager. It was a demanding role, but I thrived in it, climbing the ranks until I became the highest-ranking employee in my division in Illinois. The job came with great financial rewards, including performance bonuses that were appreciated by both me and the IRS.

As the business grew, the company decided to bring in an assistant manager to help ease my workload. Despite my hopes for some well-deserved time off, I found myself constantly fielding calls from the new assistant manager, who, unfortunately, proved to be a less-than-ideal addition to the team. He quickly ingratiated himself with corporate higher-ups, all the while undermining me behind my back and advocating for his own advancement at my expense.

Then came the budget cuts, and with them, downsizing. On an ordinary Tuesday, as FedEx delivered our weekly paychecks, I found myself blindsided. Opening my envelope revealed the words "FINAL CHECK" printed on the stub. Just like that, after six years of tireless dedication, I was suddenly unemployed, with no explanation given.

Losing my job was a devastating blow, particularly because I had invested so much of myself in it, all with the goal of providing security for my family while pursuing my entrepreneurial dreams. But amidst the shock and disappointment, I realized an important truth: nobody could fire me from my dream.

This experience served as a powerful reminder that as an entrepreneur, I am ultimately accountable to myself and my business. Just as I had diligently shown up and worked hard for a paycheck, I now needed to channel that same energy and commitment into my own venture. No longer having a traditional boss didn't mean I could afford to slack off; if anything, it meant I had to hold myself even more rigorously accountable. My business became my new boss, and I was determined to give it my all.

While some may find comfort in the perceived security of traditional employment, I had long ago made the decision that I could never work for anyone else again. Entrepreneurship, with all its challenges and uncertainties, was the path I chose, and I was determined to see it through.

GET STARTED ON YOUR DREAMS

Taking the first step is crucial in turning your dreams into reality. However, it's important to remember that success doesn't happen overnight. Just like the growth of a tree, building a successful business takes time, patience, pain and persistence.

In the initial stages, progress may seem slow, and you may encounter obstacles along the way. It's essential not to be discouraged by setbacks but instead to view them as opportunities for growth and learning.

Like the roots of a tree, the foundation of your business is paramount. Focus on laying down strong roots by investing in your skills, building relationships, and developing a solid business plan. These foundational elements will provide the stability and support needed for your business to flourish.

Stay committed to your journey, even when progress seems slow. With dedication and perseverance, your business will grow and thrive, reaching heights beyond your imagination. Remember, success is not just about the destination but also about the journey and the lessons learned along the way. Keep planting those roots, and before you know it, you'll be amazed at how far you've come.

LEARN HOW TO MAKE MISTAKES

Embracing mistakes as part of the learning process is essential for growth and success as an entrepreneur. It's through trial and error that we discover what works and what doesn't, refining our strategies along the way.

The key is to fail fast and learn quickly from those failures. By rapidly testing ideas, recording results, and analyzing feedback, you can iterate and improve your approach efficiently. This mindset allows you to adapt to challenges and setbacks with resilience, moving forward with newfound knowledge and insights.

Moreover, learning from others' mistakes can provide valuable shortcuts on your entrepreneurial journey. Leveraging the wisdom and experiences of those who have gone before you can help you avoid common pitfalls and make smarter decisions. Just pay attention and you will observe the common pitfalls of entrepreneurs.

Ultimately, the willingness to make mistakes, fail fast, and learn from both your own experiences and those of others is a powerful formula for success in entrepreneurship. It's not about avoiding failure altogether but rather about embracing it as a stepping stone to growth and innovation. Mistakes can be painful make sure that you learn from your pain.

FOCUS ON ONE PROBLEM AT A TIME

Focusing on solving one problem at a time is crucial for effective problem-solving and progress in your business endeavors. By creating a punch list or task list, you can prioritize tasks based on their deadlines and importance, ensuring that you tackle the most pressing issues first. This list should be utilized and updated daily to track your progress.

Building a strong foundation for your business is essential, just like building a house from the ground up. This means addressing fundamental issues and laying the groundwork for future growth and success.

Networking with other like-minded individuals is also invaluable. By connecting with others who may be facing similar challenges, you can gain insights, share ideas, and collaborate on finding solutions. Sometimes, someone else may have already solved a part of the problem that you haven't considered, and by sharing information, you can both benefit and move closer to resolving common issues.

Remember, progress is made one step at a time, and by focusing on solving one problem at a time, you can steadily move forward and achieve your business goals.

REMAIN OPTIMISTIC

Staying humble and being open to learning from others is crucial in the journey of entrepreneurship. No one knows everything, and there's always room for growth and improvement. By remaining humble and receptive to advice and wisdom from others, you can accelerate your learning and avoid costly mistakes.

Maintaining a positive and respectful attitude is also essential. People are more likely to collaborate and share opportunities with those who treat them with kindness and respect. Being rude or arrogant can alienate potential collaborators and hinder your progress in the industry.

Furthermore, it's important to take calculated risks in entrepreneurship. Without risk, there is no reward, and seizing opportunities often requires stepping out of your comfort zone. Whether it's performing at an open slot or collaborating with another artist, taking calculated chances can lead to valuable connections and opportunities for growth. The worst thing a potential collaborator can do is decline your request.

However, it's crucial to assess the risks and rewards of each opportunity and ensure that they align with your overall mission and goals. By being strategic and thoughtful in your decision-making, you can maximize the potential for success while minimizing potential setbacks.

CHALLENGE YOURSELF

Challenging yourself is a fundamental aspect of entrepreneurship. Stepping out of your comfort zone allows you to push your limits, discover new skills and capabilities, and ultimately grow as both a person and a business owner.

By taking on challenges that make you uncomfortable, you expand your horizons and develop resilience and adaptability in the face of uncertainty. This willingness to embrace discomfort fosters innovation and creativity, as it encourages you to explore new ideas and approaches that you may not have considered otherwise.

Moreover, overcoming challenges builds confidence and self-belief, empowering you to tackle even greater obstacles in the future. Each challenge you conquer becomes a stepping stone toward greater success, shaping you into a more resilient and resourceful entrepreneur.

Ultimately, embracing challenges is essential for personal and professional growth, as it allows you to unlock your full potential and achieve your goals. So don't shy away from discomfort—embrace it as an opportunity for growth and transformation.

BUILD A DREAM TEAM

Building a dream team in the music business is essential for achieving success and maximizing your potential. Here are some key roles to consider when assembling your team:

1. **Manager**: A skilled and experienced manager can help oversee your career, handle negotiations, book shows, manage finances, and provide valuable guidance and support.
2. **Agent**: A booking agent specializes in securing live performance opportunities for artists. They have connections with venues, promoters, and other industry professionals to help you book gigs and tours.
3. **Publicist**: A publicist helps generate publicity and media coverage for your music and brand. They pitch your music to journalists, bloggers, and influencers, arrange interviews, and manage press releases and media appearances.
4. **Producer**: A talented producer can bring your music to life and help you achieve the sound you envision. They work with you to arrange, record, and mix your songs, ensuring they meet professional standards and resonate with your audience.
5. **Songwriter**: Collaborating with skilled songwriters can enhance your music and broaden your creative horizons. They can help you craft compelling lyrics, melodies, and arrangements that resonate with listeners.
6. **Musician/Band Members**: If you're a solo artist, consider recruiting talented musicians to accompany you onstage or in the studio. If you're in a band, ensure you have dedicated and committed members who share your vision and work well together.
7. **Graphic Designer**: A graphic designer can create eye-catching album artwork, promotional materials, and merchandise designs that reflect your brand and attract fans.
8. **Social Media Manager**: An experienced social media manager can help you build and engage with your online fanbase across platforms

like Instagram, Twitter, Facebook, and TikTok. They develop content strategies, manage posting schedules, and analyze performance metrics to optimize your social media presence.

9. **Business Manager/Accountant**: A business manager or accountant helps you manage your finances, budget effectively, track income and expenses, handle taxes, and ensure compliance with financial regulations.

10. **Legal Counsel**: A music attorney provides legal advice and representation on contracts, copyright issues, licensing agreements, and other legal matters related to your music career.

By assembling a dedicated and talented team, you can leverage their expertise and support to navigate the music industry, amplify your efforts, and achieve your goals more effectively.

WORK ON YOUR PASSION AND FIND YOUR PURPOSE

Passion and purpose are crucial driving forces behind any successful venture, especially in the music business where dedication and resilience are often required. Here's why they're so important:

1. **Sustained Motivation**: When you're passionate about your business, you're more likely to stay motivated, even when faced with challenges or setbacks. Your passion fuels your determination to overcome obstacles and keep pushing forward.

2. **Resilience**: Building a career in the music industry can be tough, with rejection, criticism, and uncertainty being common experiences. However, when you're driven by passion and purpose, you're better equipped to weather these storms and bounce back stronger.

3. **Creativity and Innovation**: Passion often goes hand in hand with creativity. When you're passionate about your work, you're more likely to think outside the box, explore new ideas, and innovate in your field. This can lead to fresh and unique approaches that set you apart from the competition.

4. **Authenticity**: Passion brings authenticity to your work. When you genuinely love what you do, it shines through in your music, performances, and interactions with fans. People are drawn to authenticity, and it can help you build a loyal fanbase who connect with your genuine passion and enthusiasm.

5. **Fulfillment and Satisfaction**: Pursuing your passion brings a sense of fulfillment and satisfaction that goes beyond financial success. Knowing that you're following your dreams and making a positive impact in the world can bring a deep sense of fulfillment and happiness. This feeling is almost impossible to describe to someone who has never felt that satisfaction

6. **Longevity**: Passion and purpose provide the foundation for long-term success. When you're genuinely passionate about your work, you're more likely to stick with it through the ups and downs,

ensuring that your career has longevity and sustainability. For over two decades I have had the pleasure to work in the field that I love.

Ultimately, finding your passion and purpose in the music business is about aligning your values, interests, and talents with your career aspirations. When you're driven by passion and purpose, success becomes not just a destination but a fulfilling and rewarding journey.

BE A VISIONARY FOR YOUR LIFE

Having a clear vision for your life and career is indeed essential for success in the music business. Here's why being a visionary is important:

1. **Direction and Focus**: A vision provides you with a clear direction for where you want to go and what you want to achieve. It serves as a guiding light, helping you stay focused on your goals amidst distractions and obstacles.
2. **Motivation and Inspiration**: A compelling vision inspires you to take action and pursue your dreams with passion and determination. It fuels your motivation, especially during challenging times when you may encounter setbacks or doubts.
3. **Goal Setting**: Your vision acts as a blueprint for setting specific, achievable goals that align with your long-term aspirations. By breaking down your vision into smaller milestones, you can create actionable steps to move closer to your ultimate vision.
4. **Decision Making**: When faced with choices or opportunities, your vision serves as a decision-making tool, helping you evaluate which options are in alignment with your long-term goals and values.
5. **Resilience**: A strong vision provides you with resilience and perseverance to overcome obstacles and setbacks along the way. It reminds you of the bigger picture and motivates you to keep moving forward, even in the face of adversity.
6. **Adaptability**: While a vision provides you with a clear direction, it also allows for flexibility and adaptability as circumstances change. You can adjust your strategies and tactics while staying true to your overarching vision. Adapt and overcome is my mantra.

7. **Personal Fulfillment**: Having a vision for your life and career brings a sense of purpose and fulfillment. It gives you a sense of meaning and satisfaction, knowing that you're working towards something meaningful and impactful.

In the music business, where success often requires perseverance, creativity, and resilience, being a visionary can set you apart and help you achieve your dreams. Take the time to reflect on your aspirations, define your vision, and then take consistent action towards turning your vision into reality.

UNDERSTAND YOUR INDUSTRY AND CATER TO YOUR CONSUMERS

Understanding your industry and catering to your consumers are indeed crucial aspects of success in the music business. Here's why they are important:

1. **Industry Knowledge**: Understanding the ins and outs of the music industry allows you to navigate its complexities more effectively. This includes understanding trends, market dynamics, competition, distribution channels, and emerging technologies. By staying informed about industry developments, you can anticipate changes and adapt your strategies accordingly. This knowledge is constantly evolving and requires an adept observation of the industry and its pulse.

2. **Strategic Planning**: Armed with industry knowledge, you can develop strategic plans that capitalize on market opportunities and mitigate potential risks. This might involve identifying niche markets, forging strategic partnerships, or leveraging emerging trends to gain a competitive advantage.

3. **Targeted Marketing**: Catering to your consumers involves knowing who your target audience is and tailoring your marketing efforts to meet their needs and preferences. This might include demographic research, psychographic profiling, and analyzing consumer behavior to create targeted marketing campaigns that resonate with your audience.

4. **Building Relationships**: By understanding your industry and consumers, you can build stronger relationships with your audience, collaborators, and industry stakeholders. This might involve networking at industry events, engaging with fans on social media, or collaborating with other artists and professionals in the industry.

5. **Creating Value**: Ultimately, success in the music business comes down to creating value for your audience. Whether it's through your music, live performances, merchandise, or brand identity, you need to offer something that resonates with your audience and makes them

want to support you. Understanding your industry and consumers allows you to create and deliver value more effectively.

6. **Adaptability**: The music industry is constantly evolving, driven by technological advancements, changing consumer preferences, and industry trends. By staying informed and connected, you can adapt to these changes more quickly and position yourself for long-term success.

In summary, understanding your industry and catering to your consumers are essential components of success in the music business. By staying informed, strategic, and customer-focused, you can maximize your opportunities for growth and sustainability in a competitive and dynamic industry landscape.

ALWAYS OVERDELIVER

Overdelivering is indeed a powerful strategy for building customer loyalty and standing out in the music industry. Here's why it's important and how you can implement it effectively:

1. **Customer Satisfaction**: By exceeding customer expectations, you not only meet their needs but also delight them with unexpected value. This leads to higher levels of satisfaction and increases the likelihood of repeat business and positive word-of-mouth referrals. These referrals can be crucial to long term success.

2. **Differentiation**: In a crowded marketplace, overdelivering sets you apart from competitors who may offer similar products or services. Going above and beyond shows that you are committed to providing exceptional value and care about your customers' experience.

3. **Brand Reputation**: Consistently overdelivering builds a strong reputation for your brand as one that consistently delivers on its promises and strives to exceed customer expectations. This enhances brand trust and loyalty, which are essential for long-term success.

4. **Word-of-Mouth Marketing**: Satisfied customers are more likely to share their positive experiences with others, leading to word-of-mouth marketing and organic growth. When customers receive more value than they anticipated, they are more inclined to recommend

your music or brand to friends, family, and followers.

5. **Repeat Business**: Overdelivering fosters customer loyalty and encourages repeat business. Customers who have had positive experiences with your brand are more likely to return for future purchases and become loyal supporters of your music career.

6. **Creative Opportunities**: Overdelivering provides opportunities for creativity and innovation in how you engage with your audience. Whether it's through surprise bonuses, exclusive content, or personalized interactions, you can find unique ways to exceed expectations and leave a lasting impression.

To effectively implement the strategy of overdelivering in your music business:

- **Identify Opportunities**: Look for opportunities to add extra value at every touchpoint with your audience, whether it's through your music releases, merchandise sales, live performances, or online interactions.

- **Personalize Experiences**: Tailor your efforts to the preferences and interests of your audience. Consider their demographics, behaviors, and feedback to create personalized experiences that resonate with them on a deeper level.

- **Surprise and Delight**: Incorporate elements of surprise and delight into your interactions with fans. This could include unexpected gifts, special promotions, exclusive content, or personalized messages that show your appreciation for their support.

- **Seek Feedback**: Regularly solicit feedback from your audience to understand their needs and preferences better. Use this information to refine your approach and continue improving the value you deliver.

- **Stay Consistent**: Consistency is key to building trust and loyalty. Make overdelivering a consistent part of your brand identity and customer experience to maintain momentum and foster long-term relationships with your audience.

By prioritizing overdelivery and consistently exceeding expectations, you can cultivate a loyal fan base, differentiate yourself in the industry, and propel your music career to new heights.

PROTECT AND MONETIZE

COPYRIGHTS

Copyrights play a crucial role in the music business, protecting the intellectual property rights of songwriters, composers, performers, and other creators. Here's an overview of copyrights in the music industry:

1. **What is Copyright?**
   Copyright is a form of intellectual property law that grants creators the exclusive right to use and distribute their works for a limited period. In the music industry, copyright protects musical compositions (lyrics and melodies) and sound recordings (the actual recorded performances).
2. **Ownership of Copyright:**
   - **Musical Compositions:** The songwriter or composer typically owns the copyright to the musical composition, which includes the lyrics and melody of a song.
   - **Sound Recordings:** The owner of the sound recording copyright is usually the record label or the person or entity that financed the recording session.

1. **Rights Granted by Copyright:**
   - **Reproduction Right:** The exclusive right to make copies of the music, such as CDs, digital downloads, or vinyl records.
   - **Distribution Right:** The exclusive right to distribute copies of the music to the public.
   - **Public Performance Right:** The exclusive right to perform the music publicly, including live performances, radio broadcasts, and streaming.
   - **Adaptation Right:** The exclusive right to create derivative works based on the original music, such as remixes or cover versions.
2. **Registration of Copyright:**

While copyright protection exists automatically upon the creation of a musical work, registering the copyright with the relevant authorities provides additional benefits, such as the ability to sue for statutory damages and attorney's fees in case of infringement.

- **In the United States:** Copyright registration for musical compositions and sound recordings is handled by the U.S. Copyright Office.
- **Internationally:** Copyright protection varies by country, but many countries are signatories to international copyright treaties like the Berne Convention, which offers protection to foreign works.

3. **Licensing and Royalties:**
   - **Mechanical Licenses:** Required for reproducing and distributing musical compositions in formats like CDs, digital downloads, and streaming.
   - **Performance Licenses:** Needed for public performances of musical compositions, whether live or via broadcast, streaming services, or public venues.
   - **Sync Licenses:** Required for synchronizing music with visual media, such as films, TV shows, commercials, and video games.
   - **Royalties:** Songwriters, composers, and performers earn royalties from the use of their music, including mechanical royalties from sales and streaming, performance royalties from public performances, and sync royalties from synchronization licenses.

4. **Duration of Copyright:**
   The duration of copyright protection varies by country but typically lasts for the life of the creator plus a certain number of years (e.g., 70 years after the creator's death in many countries).

Understanding and managing copyrights are essential aspects of navigating the music business, ensuring that creators receive fair compensation for their work and protecting their artistic rights.

TRADEMARKS

Trademarks are crucial in the music business for protecting brand names, logos, slogans, and other identifiers associated with artists, bands, record labels, and music-related products and services. Here's an overview of trademarks in the music industry:

1. **What is a Trademark?**
   A trademark is a recognizable sign, design, or expression that distinguishes products or services of a particular source from those of others. It can be a word, phrase, logo, symbol, or combination thereof.
2. **Types of Trademarks:**
   - **Artist/Band Names:** Trademarking the name of a musical artist or band helps prevent others from using the same or a similar name in a way that could cause confusion among consumers.
   - **Logos and Symbols:** Visual elements like logos and symbols associated with artists, bands, or record labels can be trademarked to protect their distinctiveness.
   - **Album Titles:** While copyright protects the content of an album (e.g., songs, artwork), trademarks can protect the title of the album itself.
   - **Merchandise and Products:** Trademarks can cover merchandise bearing the artist's name or logo, such as clothing, accessories, and other branded products.
   - **Services:** Trademarks can also protect services associated with the music industry, such as concert promotion, music production, or artist management.
3. **Benefits of Trademark Registration:**
   - **Exclusive Rights:** Trademark registration provides the owner with exclusive rights to use the mark in connection with the specified goods or services.
   - **Legal Protection:** Registered trademarks are legally

presumed valid, making it easier to enforce rights against unauthorized use by others.

- **Brand Recognition:** Trademarks help build brand recognition and consumer trust by signaling the source of the products or services.
- **Asset Value:** Trademarks can have significant financial value as valuable assets of a music business, potentially increasing the company's overall worth.

4. **Trademark Registration Process:**
   - **Trademark Search:** Before applying for registration, it's essential to conduct a comprehensive trademark search to ensure that the proposed mark is available for use and registration.
   - **Application Filing:** Trademark registration applications are filed with the relevant trademark office, such as the United States Patent and Trademark Office (USPTO) in the U.S.
   - **Examination:** The trademark office examines the application to ensure that the mark meets the requirements for registration, including distinctiveness and non-confusion with existing marks.
   - **Publication:** If the application is approved, it is published for opposition, allowing third parties to challenge the registration.
   - **Registration:** If there are no oppositions or challenges, and all requirements are met, the mark is registered, providing the owner with legal protection and exclusive rights to use the mark.

5. **Trademark Infringement and Enforcement:**
   Trademark owners have the right to enforce their marks against unauthorized use by others, including through cease-and-desist letters, negotiations, and legal action, if necessary, to stop infringement and protect their brand reputation.

Trademark protection is essential for artists, bands, and music-related businesses to safeguard their brand identities, build consumer trust, and establish a competitive advantage in the music industry.

TRADE SERCRETS

Trade secrets in the music business, as in any industry, refer to valuable, confidential information that provides a competitive advantage to a music artist, band, record label, or other music-related entity. Here's an explanation of trade secrets and why they need protection in the music industry:

1. **Definition of Trade Secrets:**
   Trade secrets encompass a wide range of confidential information, including but not limited to:
       ◦ Unreleased music tracks or albums before public release.
       ◦ Exclusive contracts and agreements with collaborators, producers, or venues.
       ◦ Marketing and promotional strategies, including upcoming tour dates or album launch plans.
       ◦ Financial data, such as revenue streams, royalty agreements, and budget allocations.
       ◦ Proprietary technology or techniques used in music production, recording, or distribution.
       ◦ Customer or fan databases and contact lists.
2. **Importance of Protecting Trade Secrets:**
   Protecting trade secrets is crucial for several reasons:
       ◦ **Competitive Advantage:** Trade secrets give music businesscs a compctitive edge by providing unique insights, strategies, or resources that are not known to competitors. Keeping this information confidential helps maintain the advantage.
       ◦ **Economic Value:** Trade secrets can have significant economic value, contributing to the success and profitability of music artists, bands, and companies. Unauthorized disclosure or use by competitors can result in financial losses.

- **Brand Reputation:** Protecting trade secrets helps preserve the integrity and reputation of music brands. If sensitive information is leaked or misused, it can damage trust with collaborators, partners, and fans, leading to negative publicity and loss of goodwill.
- **Legal Protection:** While trade secrets do not require formal registration like patents or trademarks, they are protected under trade secret laws. Unauthorized acquisition, use, or disclosure of trade secrets can lead to legal action, including civil lawsuits and damages.
- **Long-Term Sustainability:** Safeguarding trade secrets is essential for the long-term sustainability of music businesses. By protecting valuable assets and confidential information, companies can maintain their competitive position and adapt to changing market conditions.

3. **Methods of Protecting Trade Secrets:**
   To protect trade secrets in the music industry, businesses can implement various strategies:

   - **Confidentiality Agreements:** Require employees, contractors, and partners to sign confidentiality or non-disclosure agreements (NDAs) to prevent unauthorized disclosure or use of confidential information.
   - **Physical Security Measures:** Implement physical security measures, such as restricted access to sensitive areas, locked storage facilities for documents or recordings, and password-protected digital files.
   - **Digital Security:** Use encryption, secure networks, access controls, and cybersecurity measures to protect digital assets and prevent unauthorized access or data breaches.
   - **Training and Education:** Provide training and education to employees and collaborators on the importance of protecting trade secrets and best practices for safeguarding confidential information.

- ○ **Monitoring and Enforcement:** Regularly monitor access to sensitive information, investigate any suspected breaches or leaks, and take appropriate enforcement action against violators.

By recognizing the value of trade secrets and implementing effective protection measures, music artists, bands, and businesses can preserve their competitive advantage, safeguard their assets, and maintain trust and credibility in the industry.

MONETIZE

Songwriters, musicians, artists, music publishers, record labels, and collection societies can make money in various ways in the music business. Here's how each of these entities typically generates revenue:

1. **Songwriters:**
   - **Mechanical Royalties:** Earned from the sale or reproduction of songs on physical media (CDs, vinyl) or digital downloads and streams.
   - **Performance Royalties:** Earned when songs are performed or broadcast publicly, such as on radio, TV, in live performances, or through digital streaming services.
   - **Sync Licensing:** Generated from licensing songs for use in movies, TV shows, commercials, video games, and other media productions.
   - **Publishing Royalties:** Derived from ownership of the publishing rights to songs, often shared with music publishers.
2. **Musicians/Artists:**
   - **Live Performances:** Revenue from ticket sales, merchandise sales (e.g., T-shirts, posters), and performance fees for live concerts, festivals, and tours.
   - **Merchandise Sales:** Income from selling branded merchandise, including clothing, accessories, and memorabilia.
   - **Digital Sales and Streaming:** Royalties earned from digital downloads, streams, and purchases of music on platforms like iTunes, Spotify, Apple Music, and others.
   - **Physical Sales:** Revenue from sales of physical music formats, such as CDs, vinyl records, and cassette tapes.
3. **Music Publishers:**
   - **Publishing Royalties:** Earned from the ownership and

administration of song copyrights, including mechanical royalties, performance royalties, and sync licensing fees.

- **Sub-Publishing:** Income generated from licensing songs in foreign territories through sub-publishing agreements with international partners.
- **Administration Fees:** Charges for providing administrative services to songwriters, such as copyright registration, royalty collection, and licensing.

1. **Record Labels:**
   - **Record Sales:** Revenue from sales of physical and digital recordings, including CDs, vinyl, downloads, and streams, after deducting manufacturing and distribution costs.
   - **Artist Advances:** Payments made to artists as advances against future earnings from record sales, tours, and other revenue streams.
   - **Licensing and Distribution Deals:** Income from licensing recordings to other labels, distributors, or streaming platforms for distribution.
   - **Merchandising and Brand Partnerships:** Revenue from merchandise sales, brand partnerships, sponsorships, and endorsements related to artists signed to the label.
2. **Collection Societies:**
   - **Performance Royalties:** Collected on behalf of songwriters and publishers from public performances, broadcasts, and digital streams of music.
   - **Mechanical Royalties:** Collected from record labels, streaming services, and other music users for the reproduction and distribution of songs.
   - **Sync Licensing Fees:** Collected for the licensing of songs for use in film, TV, commercials, and other media productions.

- **International Royalties:** Collected from foreign collection societies for performances and uses of music in international territories.

ADVERTISING MONETIZATION

Advertising monetization is a strategy used by content creators, including musicians and music distributors, to generate revenue by displaying advertisements alongside their content. In the context of the music business, advertising monetization typically involves displaying ads on websites, streaming platforms, social media channels, and other digital platforms where music is distributed or promoted. Here's how advertising monetization works:

1. **Ad Placement:** Content creators, such as musicians or music distributors, allow third-party advertisers to display ads alongside their content. These ads can take various forms, including display ads, video ads, audio ads, sponsored content, and native advertising.

2. **Ad Networks and Platforms:** Content creators partner with ad networks or advertising platforms that connect them with advertisers looking to reach their target audience. These ad networks facilitate the placement of ads on the content creator's platform or website and manage the advertising process, including ad serving, tracking, and revenue collection.

3. **Monetization Models:** Advertising monetization can follow different monetization models, including:
   - Cost per Impression (CPM): Advertisers pay a fixed amount for every thousand impressions (views) of their ad.
   - Cost per Click (CPC): Advertisers pay a fee each time a user clicks on their ad.
   - Cost per Action (CPA): Advertisers pay a fee when a specific action is completed, such as signing up for a newsletter or making a purchase.

4. **Revenue Sharing:** In many cases, content creators receive a share of the advertising revenue generated by their content. The ad network or platform typically handles revenue sharing arrangements, with

content creators receiving a percentage of the ad revenue based on factors such as ad impressions, clicks, or actions.

5. **Targeted Advertising:** Advertisers can target their ads to specific audiences based on demographics, interests, behavior, and other factors. This targeted advertising allows advertisers to reach users who are more likely to be interested in their products or services, resulting in higher ad engagement and revenue potential for content creators.

6. **Ad Formats:** Advertisers can choose from various ad formats to reach their target audience, including:

    ◦ Display Ads: Visual ads that appear on websites, social media platforms, and mobile apps.

    ◦ Video Ads: Short video clips that play before, during, or after music videos, livestreams, or other video content.

    ◦ Audio Ads: Audio commercials that play during music streaming sessions or podcasts.

    ◦ Native Ads: Advertisements that blend seamlessly with the surrounding content, appearing as sponsored posts or recommendations.

Overall, advertising monetization provides content creators in the music business with an additional revenue stream by allowing them to earn money from advertisements displayed alongside their music content. By partnering with ad networks and platforms, content creators can reach a broader audience and monetize their music effectively through targeted advertising campaigns.

YouTube:

1. **YouTube Partner Program (YPP):** Content creators can join the YouTube Partner Program to monetize their videos through advertising. To qualify for the program, creators must meet certain eligibility requirements, including having at least 1,000 subscribers and 4,000 watch hours in the past 12 months.

2. **Ad Formats:** YouTube offers various ad formats, including pre-roll ads (played before the video), mid-roll ads (played during the video), and overlay ads (displayed as banners on the video player).

3. **Monetization Models:** Creators earn revenue based on the number of ad views and clicks generated by their videos. YouTube shares a portion of the advertising revenue with creators through its AdSense program.
4. **Targeting Options:** Advertisers can target their ads on YouTube based on factors such as demographics, interests, and viewing behavior, ensuring that ads are shown to relevant audiences.

Facebook:

1. **Facebook Ad Breaks:** Content creators can monetize their videos on Facebook through Ad Breaks, which allow ads to be inserted into eligible videos. Creators must meet certain eligibility criteria, such as having at least 10,000 followers and generating at least 30,000 one-minute views on videos that are at least 3 minutes long in the past 60 days.
2. **Ad Formats:** Facebook offers various ad formats, including in-stream ads (played during the video), pre-roll ads, mid-roll ads, and image ads displayed in the News Feed or Stories.
3. **Monetization Models:** Similar to YouTube, creators earn revenue based on ad views and clicks generated by their videos. Facebook shares a portion of the advertising revenue with creators.
4. **Audience Targeting:** Advertisers can target their ads on Facebook based on factors such as demographics, interests, behavior, and location, allowing for precise audience targeting.

Instagram:

1. **Instagram Ads:** Content creators can monetize their content on Instagram by partnering with brands for sponsored posts or by using Instagram's advertising platform to promote their content.
2. **Ad Formats:** Instagram offers various ad formats, including photo ads, video ads, carousel ads (multiple images or videos in one post), and Stories ads (full-screen ads displayed between users' Stories).
3. **Monetization Models:** Creators can earn revenue through

sponsored content deals with brands, where they promote products or services in their posts. Alternatively, creators can use Instagram's advertising platform to run paid ad campaigns and reach a broader audience.

4. **Audience Targeting:** Instagram provides robust audience targeting options, allowing advertisers to target their ads based on demographics, interests, behavior, and more.

How to Get Started:

1. **Join Monetization Programs:** Follow the guidelines and eligibility requirements to join the monetization programs offered by each platform (e.g., YouTube Partner Program, Facebook Ad Breaks).
2. **Create Engaging Content:** Produce high-quality, engaging content that attracts viewers and encourages them to watch, like, and share your videos.
3. **Enable Monetization Features:** Enable monetization features on your account and videos to start displaying ads and earning revenue.
4. **Promote Your Content:** Promote your videos across social media platforms, engage with your audience, and encourage them to watch and interact with your content to increase ad revenue.
5. **Optimize for Audience Engagement:** Focus on creating content that resonates with your target audience to maximize views, engagement, and ad revenue.

By leveraging advertising monetization on platforms like YouTube, Facebook, and Instagram, content creators in the music industry can generate revenue from their music videos, reach a wider audience, and grow their fan base while pursuing their passion.

Overall, the music business offers multiple revenue streams for various stakeholders, including creators, rights holders, publishers, labels, and collection societies, each deriving income from different sources within the industry ecosystem.

MUSIC DISTRIBUTION

Music distribution refers to the process of making music available to consumers through various channels such as physical retail, digital downloads, streaming platforms, and other media outlets. It involves getting music from artists, record labels, or distributors to retailers, streaming services, and ultimately to the end consumers.

Major Distribution: Major distribution typically involves deals with major record labels or distribution companies that have significant resources, industry connections, and market reach. These companies often handle distribution for well-established artists and labels and have the infrastructure to promote and distribute music on a large scale.

Examples of major distribution companies include:

1. **Universal Music Group Distribution:**
   - **Website:** UMG[1]
   - **Contact Information:** Visit their website for contact details.
2. **Sony Music Entertainment Distribution:**
   - **Website:** Sony Music[2]
   - **Contact Information:** Available on their website.
3. **Warner Music Group Distribution:**
   - **Website:** Warner Music Group[3]
   - **Contact Information:** Provided on their website.

Major distribution deals often come with significant financial backing, extensive marketing and promotional support, and access to a wide network of retailers, streaming platforms, and media outlets. However, they may also involve stricter contractual terms and higher fees or revenue splits.

---

1. https://www.universalmusic.com/

2. https://www.sonymusic.com/

3. https://www.wmg.com/

Independent Distribution: Independent distribution refers to distribution deals with smaller, independent distribution companies or DIY (do-it-yourself) methods employed by artists or small labels to distribute their music without major label involvement. Independent distribution allows artists to retain more control over their music and finances but may require more effort in terms of marketing and promotion.

Examples of independent distribution companies include:

1. **CD Baby:**
   - **Website:** CD Baby[4]
   - **Contact Information:** Visit their website for contact details.
2. **TuneCore:**
   - **Website:** TuneCore[5]
   - **Contact Information:** Available on their website.
3. **DistroKid:**
   - **Website:** DistroKid[6]
   - **Contact Information:** Provided on their website.

Independent distribution platforms often offer user-friendly interfaces, affordable pricing options, and access to a wide range of digital retailers and streaming services. Artists and labels can upload their music directly to these platforms, which then distribute it to online stores and streaming platforms worldwide. My company Urban Grind TV provides music and video distribution via our UGTV Distro division. You can lean more at UrbanGrindTV.com[7]

SCAN CODE FOR MUSIC DISTRO:

---

4. https://cdbaby.com/

5. https://www.tunecore.com/

6. https://distrokid.com/

7. https://urbangrindtv.com/

In summary, major distribution offers extensive resources and industry connections but may involve stricter terms, while independent distribution provides more control and flexibility but requires artists to take on more responsibility for marketing and promotion. Artists and labels should choose the distribution option that best aligns with their goals, budget, and level of independence.

MUSIC DISTRIBUTION PROCESS

The music distribution process involves several steps to get music from artists, record labels, or distributors to retailers, streaming services, and ultimately to the end consumers. Here's an overview of the typical music distribution process:

1. **Content Preparation:**
   - Artists or record labels prepare their music for distribution by ensuring it meets technical specifications and quality standards. This includes mastering the audio, creating artwork for album covers, and organizing metadata such as track titles, artist names, and album information.

1. **Choosing a Distribution Channel:**
   - Artists or labels decide on the distribution channels they want to use, which may include physical retail, digital downloads, streaming platforms, or a combination of these. They may opt for major distribution deals with record labels or independent distribution through online platforms.
2. **Distribution Agreement.**
   - Artists or labels negotiate and sign distribution agreements with distribution companies or platforms. These agreements outline the terms and conditions of distribution, including revenue splits, fees, territory rights, and promotional support.
3. **Content Delivery:**

- Artists or labels deliver their music content to the distribution company or platform according to the specifications outlined in the distribution agreement. This may involve uploading digital files, delivering physical copies of CDs or vinyl records, or providing access to master recordings.

4. **Metadata Entry:**
   - Metadata such as track titles, artist names, album information, genre classifications, and release dates are entered into the distribution system. This metadata helps organize and categorize music for retailers, streaming platforms, and consumers.

5. **Distribution to Retailers and Streaming Platforms:**
   - The distribution company or platform distributes the music to various retailers, streaming services, and media outlets. This may include online stores, digital download platforms, streaming platforms like Spotify or Apple Music, radio stations, and physical retailers.

6. **Promotion and Marketing:**
   - Artists, labels, or distribution partners engage in promotional activities to generate awareness and drive sales or streams of the music. This may include marketing campaigns, advertising, social media promotion, press releases, radio play, playlist placements, and live performances.

7. **Sales and Royalties:**
   - Music is sold or streamed through retail channels, and royalties are collected based on the distribution agreement and applicable copyright laws. Revenue generated from sales, streams, and other uses of the music is distributed to artists, labels, songwriters, and other rights holders according to their contractual arrangements.

8. **Reporting and Analytics:**
   - Distribution companies or platforms provide artists and labels with reports and analytics on the performance of their

music, including sales figures, streaming data, audience demographics, and revenue earned. This information helps artists and labels track their success and make informed decisions about their music distribution strategies.

Overall, the music distribution process involves collaboration between artists, labels, distributors, retailers, streaming platforms, and other stakeholders to bring music to audiences worldwide. Each step of the process plays a crucial role in ensuring the success of the music and maximizing its reach and impact.

GET PAID FROM MUSIC DISTRIBUTION

Getting paid from music distribution involves several steps, depending on the distribution channels used and the agreements in place between artists, record labels, and distribution companies. Here's a general overview of how artists can get paid from music distribution:

1. **Sales Revenue:**
   - When music is sold through retail channels such as online stores, physical retailers, or direct-to-fan platforms, artists earn revenue based on the sales of their music. This revenue may come from sales of digital downloads, physical copies (CDs, vinyl), or merchandise bundles that include music.

2. **Streaming Revenue:**
   - Artists earn revenue from music streaming platforms based on the number of streams their songs receive. Streaming services pay royalties to rights holders (artists, songwriters, labels) based on factors such as the number of streams, the territory of the listener, and the type of subscription (premium, ad-supported).

3. **Royalty Payments:**
   - Artists receive royalty payments from distribution companies or record labels based on the terms of their distribution agreements. These royalties may be calculated as a percentage of net revenue earned from sales and streams, and they may be subject to deductions for distribution fees,

marketing costs, and other expenses.

4. **Performance Royalties:**
    - Artists earn performance royalties when their music is played on radio, TV, or public performances such as live concerts, festivals, and events. Performance rights organizations (PROs) collect these royalties on behalf of artists and songwriters and distribute them based on usage data and royalty agreements.

5. **Sync Licensing Revenue:**
    - Artists may earn revenue from sync licensing, which involves licensing their music for use in film, TV, commercials, video games, and other media projects. Artists receive upfront payments and/or ongoing royalties for the use of their music in these sync placements.

6. **Direct Sales and Merchandise:**
    - Artists can generate revenue from direct sales of music and merchandise through their own websites, online stores, or at live performances. Revenue from these sales goes directly to the artist, minus any costs associated with production, fulfillment, and shipping.

7. **Accounting and Reporting:**
    - Distribution companies, record labels, and collection societies provide artists with accounting statements and reports detailing their earnings from music distribution. These statements typically include information on sales, streams, royalties, deductions, and other income sources.

1. **Payment Distribution:**
    - Artists receive payments from distribution companies, record labels, PROs, and other sources based on their earnings from music distribution. Payments may be made on a regular schedule (e.g., monthly, quarterly) and may be distributed via bank transfer, check, or electronic payment methods.

Overall, getting paid from music distribution involves understanding the various revenue streams, royalty structures, and payment processes involved in the music industry. Artists should carefully review their distribution agreements, track their earnings, and work with trusted partners to ensure they receive fair compensation for their music.

FAREWELL

As we conclude "Music is My Business: The Ultimate Start-Up Guide to the Music Industry," remember this:

In the vast landscape of the music industry, your journey is uniquely yours. From the first chords strummed to the final mix mastered, every step is a testament to your passion, dedication, and unwavering pursuit of your dreams.

As you navigate the complexities of entrepreneurship in the music business, keep these principles close to heart: innovate relentlessly, collaborate generously, and never underestimate the power of resilience.

Embrace the challenges as opportunities for growth, and let each setback fuel your determination to rise higher. Surround yourself with a dream team of mentors, collaborators, and supporters who uplift and inspire you to reach new heights.

With every beat, every lyric, and every melody, you're shaping not just your career but the very essence of your legacy. So, stand tall, stay true to your vision, and let the music you create resonate far and wide.

As you embark on this exhilarating journey, may "Music is My Business" be your trusted companion, guiding you through the highs and lows with wisdom, insight, and a steadfast belief in the power of your artistry.

Now, go forth and make your mark on the world. The stage is set, the spotlight awaits, and the symphony of success is yours to conduct. Dream boldly, create passionately, and let the music of your business echo for generations to come.

Thank you for embarking on this journey with us. Your story is just beginning, and the world eagerly awaits the melody only you can play.

Wally Lockard III J.D.

Don't miss out!

Visit the website below and you can sign up to receive emails whenever Wally Lockard III publishes a new book. There's no charge and no obligation.

https://books2read.com/r/B-A-DZANB-GPUJD

BOOKS 2 READ

Connecting independent readers to independent writers.

About the Author

Wally Lockard III, J.D., a renowned figure from Chicago, boasts over two decades of influence in the entertainment industry. With expertise spanning music, management, television, and media, he's made a lasting impact on urban culture.

A standout achievement is his stewardship of Urban Grind TV (UGTV), a revered Hip-Hop show running for 15 years and 28 seasons on Comcast Cable 25 in Chicago. As its Executive Producer, he's lauded for his visionary leadership, earning the show 26 awards.

Apart from UGTV, Wally has guided music artists to chart success, with placements on the iTunes Top 10 and Billboard Charts, reaching as high as #19. His dedication to showcasing emerging talent and expanding creative boundaries is evident across ventures like Urban Grind Radio, UGTV Music Distro, UGTV Latino, and UGTV Models.

Under Urban Grind Management, Wally leverages his expertise to guide talent and drive innovation. His commitment to education and mentorship is evident through involvement in organizations like the Chicago Music Awards and the Recording Academy. He also contributes to the Triton College Alumni Association.

As Vice President of Operations for Kingz Kounty Media Group in Brooklyn, NY, Wally continues to shape the industry. His military service and induction into the Hip-Hop Heritage Foundation Hall of Fame further highlight his impact.

For updates from Wally Lockard III and Urban Grind Management, visit UrbanGrindTV.com or follow @UrbanGrindTV on social media.

Read more at https://urbangrindtv.com/.